THE GLA

Ryan Craig

THE GLASS ROOM

OBERON BOOKS
LONDON

First published in 2006 by Oberon Books Ltd
521 Caledonian Road, London N7 9RH
Tel: 020 7607 3637 / Fax: 020 7607 3629
e-mail: info@oberonbooks.com
www.oberonbooks.com

A catalogue record for this book is available from the British
Library.

ISBN: 1 84002 712 6 / 978-1-84002-712-9

Printed in Great Britain by Antony Rowe Ltd, Chippenham

for Rebecca

If we don't believe in freedom of expression for people we despise, we don't believe in it at all.
NOAM CHOMSKY

Freedom of speech was the greatest safety, because if a man is a fool the best thing to do is to encourage him to advertise the fact by speaking.
WOODROW WILSON

Characters

MYLES, thirties

TARA, twenties

PETE, fifties

ELENA, fifties

Setting: London

Time: 2006

The symbol ' / ' is sometimes used to denote the
point at which the next speaker interrupts.

The Glass Room was first performed on 23 November 2006 at the Hampstead Theatre, London, with the following company:

MYLES, Daniel Weyman
TARA, Emma Cunniffe
PETE, Toby Salaman
ELENA, Sian Thomas

Director Anthony Clark
Designer Ruari Murchison
Lighting Designer Johanna Town
Sound Designer Gregory Clarke
Assistant Director Noah Birksted-Breen
Production Manager Tom Albu
Company Stage Manager Lorna Seymour
Deputy Stage Manager Lucy Harkness
Assistant Stage Manager Ruth McMeel

Act One

SCENE ONE

Room in a flat in central London.

MYLES enters carrying a smallish cardboard box full of books, files, CDs etc. Balancing on top of the box is a chessboard. He looks about the fairly empty room and takes it in. This will be his new home. He is hoping that no one is about.

MYLES: Hello?

    TARA enters in a pair of tatty dungarees. She has been painting.

TARA: Hi.

MYLES: Hi. I didn't think you'd be in.

TARA: I am.

MYLES: You're red.

TARA: Actually it's Tequila Sunrise.

MYLES: Right.

TARA: I was painting your room.

MYLES: Tequila Sunrise?

TARA: It's a sort of vermillion. I hope you like it.

MYLES: I'm sorry, it's all been very quick hasn't it? Just things at my last place…got complicated. What I mean is I don't know how long I'll need the room…

TARA: Oh. You hate it.

MYLES: No. What?

TARA: You've barely walked over the threshold and you're already talking about moving out.

MYLES: I move a lot. I'm always… I never stay in one place for too long.

TARA: There's a word for that.

MYLES: Peripatetic.

TARA: Good word.

MYLES: Thanks. Mind if I put this…

TARA: Please.

MYLES puts down the box. Then he takes the chessboard off the top of the box.

Do you play?

MYLES: A little.

TARA: I bet you're a grand mufti.

MYLES: Master. Hardly. I'll teach you if you like?

TARA: Teach me?

MYLES: If you like.

Awkward pause.

TARA: So. Here you are then.

MYLES: Here I am.

TARA: But be honest, it's the vermillion isn't it? You hate the vermillion.

MYLES: No I love the vermillion.

TARA: Really?

MYLES: Absolutely. It's my favourite hue. It's bright, it's ebullient…

TARA: Oh God, you really hate it.

MYLES: I love it. Honestly. Please…

TARA: The truth is...the heating doesn't really work in your room, so I thought if I paint it a really, you know, warm colour, you might not notice.

MYLES: Why don't I see for myself?

TARA: Brilliant.

MYLES goes off. TARA flicks through his CDs.

(*Shouting off.*) Is it all right?!

MYLES: (*Off.*) I love it.

TARA: It doesn't make you want to vomit or anything?

MYLES returns. He watches her looking at his things. She looks at him, finally.

MYLES: Not at all. I love it.

TARA: It's sweet of you to lie. (*Before he can respond.*) This your CD collection?

MYLES: Why? No good?

TARA: Arctic Monkeys. Coldplay. Snow Patrol. It's a pretty frosty assortment.

MYLES: I never thought about it like that. I just get what I'm told.

TARA: What you're told?

MYLES: By society. For my demographic. Age, gender, race, learning.

TARA: That's extremely sad.

MYLES: I've got some Arvo Part.

TARA: Is that a band?

MYLES: It's a... He's a composer. I'll show you.

TARA: Please don't.

MYLES: Right. So I should say…you know…thanks for choosing me…you must have had loads of applicants. It's such an excellent location. I'm flattered I came out on top.

TARA: Yeah. Oh well, I mean, you know, with my track record I didn't want to live with anyone I found attractive or anything, you know, you never know what'll happen.

MYLES: Right. Well, so, that's good then…

TARA: Oh no I don't mean…not that you're not attractive.

MYLES: OK.

TARA: Just that you're not my type.

MYLES: Excellent.

TARA: I like chunky men.

MYLES: That's a relief then.

TARA: So there's no danger of…you know…

MYLES: Totally.

TARA: …winter nights…too much red wine…

MYLES: Very sensible.

TARA: And what with you being a lawyer. Sorry, no offence or anything, but…

MYLES: I totally understand….

TARA: I usually go for the off-the-wall types. All ego and hair mousse and lots of friends who are girls and who they confide in. Your general nightmare.

MYLES: Is it? Is it?

TARA: Oh yes. And I don't really get along with passionless, lawyer boys from public schools with their severe collars, d'you know what I mean?

MYLES: Intimately.

TARA: I mean I don't mean to be rude, you know, not to your face…

MYLES: You obviously feel strongly about…

TARA: I mean I'm sure you're really passionate and wacky.

MYLES: I'm not even a tiny bit wacky.

TARA: All the guffawing and the rugby and the sodomy, it's not for me.

MYLES: Right…

TARA: Plus I'd only aggravate them.

MYLES: Probably.

TARA: (*Beat.*) Just…

MYLES: Oh. I mean…I don't mean…

TARA: …I needed the cash you see. The job doesn't pay much. I needed to get in a lodger. But I want to make a break for it. Do something more…you know. Be part of the solution, not the problem. No offence. Again.

MYLES: OK.

TARA: So it suits me that you won't be here long.

MYLES: You said something about being a writer.

TARA: God no. Well. Sort of. I write for the *Daily Mirror*. I know it's a bit…

MYLES: No, no. My Dad's a big fan. He swears by it.

TARA: Oh.

MYLES: Never misses an issue.

TARA: I do the agony aunt letters.

MYLES: Oh.

TARA: What?

MYLES: No I just…I assumed they were made up.

TARA: They are. By me. Then the agony aunt does the response.

MYLES: Right. So you're the agony rather than the aunt.

TARA: Exactly.

MYLES: But you must get real letters?

TARA: Oh yes. But my editor prefers the made up version. People have a pretty hard time with the truth.

MYLES smiles.

You're smiling at me.

MYLES: Yes.

TARA smiles. The buzzer sounds.

It'll be my Dad.

TARA: (*Into intercom.*) Hello.

PETE: (*On intercom.*) Pete Brody.

TARA: (*Buzzes him in.*) Come up.

MYLES: You must have to dispense a lot of agony to pay for this place.

TARA: The flat was left to me. My husband.

MYLES: Right. Did you and he… Sorry I'm prying…

TARA: No, no, it's fine. It's in your nature to probe.

MYLES: That's true.

TARA: Probe away.

MYLES: What happened?

TARA: Dead.

MYLES: Oh.

TARA: Yes.

MYLES: God. I'm…

TARA: Well. Not dead exactly.

MYLES: …oh. Right. I'm not sure I…

TARA: Alive really…but living in Wales.

MYLES: I see.

TARA: With a Welsh woman. Lovely…Welsh…woman.

MYLES: You divorced?

TARA: Yes but it's all fine. I've got a boyfriend so it's completely fine.

MYLES: Great.

TARA: Oh yes, a very serious boyfriend. Who I love very much.

MYLES: Chunky? Is he?

TARA: Very.

MYLES: Fantastic.

TARA: Yes, actually it is fantastic.

PETE enters with pillows and duvets and stuff, and dumps it on the floor with a groan.

PETE: I'm sweating like a new recruit in Basra.

MYLES: That's a two-journey load, Dad.

TARA: Hello.

PETE is a little taken aback by the sight of TARA.

PETE: Pete Brody.

PETE puts out his hand. She shows the red hand.

TARA: Covered in paint. I'm Tara.

PETE: Right. You've been painting.

MYLES: (*Sarcastic.*) That'll explain it then.

PETE: (*Suspicious.*)This…uh…this your place then?

TARA: Yes. All mine.

PETE: So you're saying you own it?

TARA: Yes. I'm the landlady.

PETE: I see.

MYLES: It's a great spot.

PETE: That's why the kid took it. It's near his office.

TARA: Yes he said; when he came to look round.

PETE: Yes. Very handy for the kid. That's the main reason he would have plumped for this premises. So you live here too do you?

TARA: (*Sensing his unease.*) Uh…yes…

PETE: So it'll be the two of you. You and the kid.

MYLES: (*To PETE.*) I'm thirty-one. (*To TARA.*) I'm thirty-one.

TARA: Did you get here all right?

PETE: Nope.

TARA: Oh.

PETE: Terrible journey. Bugger to get to from Cannon's Park.

MYLES: There's a march on today. The roads were all clogged up.

TARA: Oh yes the one against the anti-Islamic cartoons.

PETE: Actually it's a march against the march against the anti-Islamic cartoons.

TARA: Who'd have thought a few little cartoons in a newspaper in Denmark would cause such a fuss?

PETE: A fuss? A fuss?

TARA: Well…

MYLES: Here we go.

PETE: It's a lot more than a fuss sweetheart, it's a global bloody inferno. Did you know a student newspaper, in this country, a student newspaper that ran the Danish cartoons…

MYLES: He's off. You've encouraged him.

PETE: Pulped. The whole bleedin' lot. Then, a couple of days ago, a magazine based in London had the cartoons on their website. Staff got death threats. Police told them there was nothing they could do to protect them, so they had to take them off. Now that would be fine, except that on our way here, and this mind you is only a few days after these events, the whole place is teeming with police. They said on the radio – I enjoy that Talk Radio, gets the blood flowing – just now, on air…five hundred officers to protect the Muslim march. It's holding up the whole of central London. What's that all about?

TARA: Well…

PETE: I can't complain I suppose, the police are pretty good about protecting the synagogue where I pray. We're Jewish. I suppose Myles told you.

TARA: No.

PETE: No?

MYLES: Of course I didn't.

PETE: Oh well, that's the fact of it. There we are. Not a problem for you is it? The Jewish thing?

TARA: A problem?

PETE: Just checking. Some people are a bit anti, know what I mean?

TARA: Not me.

PETE: It's a bizarre world.

TARA: A Jewish lady taught me the flute.

PETE: We are a musical people, no doubt about it.

TARA: (*Looking at MYLES.*) Some of you anyway.

PETE: Anyway my point is there's this magazine, an organ, if you will, of free speech, under threat, but where are the forces of law and order to protect them? Oh they have no problem protecting these maniacs on the first march going around threatening to butcher people, carve 'em up.

TARA: That must have been scary.

MYLES: He should know. He was there.

TARA: No.

PETE: I was.

TARA: Why?

PETE: Went down there to give them a piece of my mind.

MYLES: Very intelligent.

TARA: What happened?

PETE: I got bloody nicked didn't I?

TARA: You didn't?

PETE: Public Order offence if you don't mind. I was standing there watching these lunatics foaming at the mouth, screaming blue murder, threatening people with execution and me an NHS nurse, a servant of the nation's health, I get banged up. The kid here had to come down and get me out.

TARA: Well done kid.

MYLES glares at TARA, who is smiling cheekily back.

PETE: Not that I got anything against the Muslim people. No way. I got a lot of Islamist friends down the Edgware General. All kinds of nationalities. Hard-working people. Dedicated to their family. But that behaviour, I'm sorry, it's unacceptable. That's why I went down there that day to the march. Have a go. Stand up to be counted.

TARA: You sound like a man of principles.

PETE: That's because I am one.

MYLES: And which of these principles were you exercising that day Dad?

PETE: My belief in the right of each citizen to express his displeasure free from fetters.

MYLES: Displeasure at what?

PETE: At the attack on free speech which was so brutally displayed that day in the streets of my home town.

MYLES: So by defending the free speech of one group you attacked the free speech of another?

PETE: Free speech? Threatening to kill is not free speech.

MYLES: Only a few people had placards like that. Most were there to express their offence, which they have every right under the law so to do.

PETE: Listen to the human rights lawyer.

MYLES: So you could see attacking that right as an attack on freedom of speech.

PETE: Oh so you think anyone should be allowed to say whatever the hell they want?

MYLES: I don't say anything…

PETE: You never do.

MYLES: I'm just saying…

PETE: What about these newspapers in Iran printing these cartoons of the Holocaust in response? You think they should be allowed to do that?

MYLES: It's the same thing. How can you protect the right of the Danish newspaper to print their cartoons, and attack the rights of the Iranians to print theirs?

PETE: Because it offends me! It offends me as an Englishman and it offends me as a Jew. And it should offend you for the same reason.

MYLES: Dad…

PETE: But you're in denial aren't you. You deny your Jewishness.

MYLES: I don't deny it, it just isn't a thing.

PETE: (*To TARA.*) I bought him books. Wonderful books.

MYLES: You're still going on about these books?

PETE: Books about his heritage. Books about his people. Never even opened them.

MYLES: I was twelve.

PETE: Telling him all about where we come from.

TARA: Cannon's Park.

PETE: Pardon me?

TARA: Cannon's Park. You said…

PETE: Yes.

TARA: I don't know it.

PETE: Just off the A5. North-west London.

TARA: It sounds a magical place.

PETE: Yeah?

Silence.

TARA: I'd better get back to the painting.

TARA goes. PETE waits for her to be out of earshot.

PETE: She's female.

MYLES: Oh you noticed that too.

PETE: You know what I mean.

MYLES: Not really.

PETE: You think that's a good idea? Sharing with a young woman of connubial proportions.

MYLES: Jesus…Dad…

PETE: I mean considering?

MYLES: Look…

PETE: I don't know if I approve.

MYLES: I won't be here long.

PETE: I mean, you don't know this girl from a bar of soap.

MYLES: It's nothing to do with you.

PETE: You kept schtum about that one. I don't know what's going on with you anymore. You don't talk to me.

MYLES: You didn't have to help me.

PETE: I know you talk to your Mum about things, but I'm here as well. But you never even talk to me about your work. And I know you're involved in sensitive cases. Important cases. With the Home Office. And you got your Mum to talk to, I know that, I appreciate that… But I'm your Dad…

MYLES: I know.

PETE: So when are you gonna talk to me?

Pause.

21

MYLES: Let's crack on with the shifting shall we?

They go. TARA comes back. She sneakily looks in the bag, pulls out a shirt with a big stiff collar and looks at it, smelling it. Lights dim to black.

SCENE TWO

Safe-house in a London suburb. Study. Some months later.

It is late spring. Afternoon. ELENA has her back to the audience. She is smoking. She is talking to someone off, quite exercised and upbeat.

ELENA: ...that tree outside, the one in the driveway as we came in, that's a laburnum. In the summer it'll be covered in a sort of wispy bright yellow bloom. You can extract venom from the flower you know?! It's skeletal in the winter, naked in the cold, but in the summer it blossoms into a magnificent and golden...magnificent and poisonous. I told the policeman. He said the wood's good for making guitars. Apparently he's an aficionado. He's got his own workshop in his garage. Did you know his name was Potts? P C Potts.

She starts looking around the room, picking up objects for the first time.

At least they let me smoke in here. More than they do on the outside.

ELENA stubs out her cigarette. The toilet flushes and a door unlocks.

I'm sure P C Potts will be making a note of every cigarette in his little book. He's 'keeping an eye on me'. But I suppose it's better than the alternative. I never thanked you for getting me off remand. This place. It's very grand.

MYLES enters.

22

MYLES: The loo's got gold leaf on the flush. God I'm a good lawyer.

ELENA: Did you hear anything I said?

MYLES: Sorry I had the taps running…

ELENA: Potts.

MYLES: The policeman?

ELENA: He makes guitars in his garage. Out of laburnum trees.

MYLES: Right.

Beat. He goes to a desk in the centre of the room and leafs through an enormous file.

ELENA: The other one…

MYLES: W P C Marjoram.

ELENA: She's a little sour faced don't you think?

MYLES: I asked her about the surveillance cameras and she told me it was none of my concern. Then as I'm walking off she goes, 'I've got no tolerance for lawyers. Just so we understand each other.'

ELENA: Terrifying.

MYLES: And Potts makes guitars you say?

ELENA: You wait those two'll have their own TV show by the end of the year.

MYLES: Yeah. So, look, I'm afraid we have to go through your statement before you get settled in and all that. I think I found an anomaly.

ELENA: Did you know we can't say 'brain storming'?

MYLES: I just want to eliminate it as a factor. (*Scans the documents.*)

23

ELENA: I was talking about ideas, coming up with ideas, you know, for my defence, and I used the phrase 'brain storming'. 'Let's brain storm' or something.

MYLES: Hmm.

ELENA: And I was ticked off. We have to say 'thought shower' instead. It offends the epileptics you see. Apparently 'brain storming' is what happens to them when they have one of their fits.

MYLES: (*Finally looking up.*) Fits?

ELENA: Yes, you know: (*She flaps her hands a little and winces.*)

MYLES: Sorry, what?

ELENA: The epileptics.

MYLES: I missed something, when were we talking about epileptics?

ELENA: I mean political correctness.

MYLES: Yes?

ELENA: I mean the culture of political correctness that makes us all live like criminals.

MYLES: Oh that.

ELENA: So we mustn't say 'brain storm'. We have to say 'thought shower'.

MYLES: Right. Who ticked you off about it?

ELENA: What?

MYLES: Who have you been speaking to?

ELENA: On the phone, I…

MYLES: Who were you speaking to on the phone? You're not supposed / to…

ELENA: All right, I didn't know I was under house arrest.

MYLES: (*Amazed.*) You didn't know you were under house arrest?

ELENA: I'm joking. Of course I know I'm under house arrest, I was being sarcastic.

MYLES: I'm not good at picking up on sarcasm, I went to public school.

ELENA: Was that a sarcastic comment about sarcasm?

MYLES: … Sort of.

ELENA: Very post-modern.

MYLES: Thanks.

ELENA: It wasn't a compliment.

MYLES: Your phone calls are supposed to be approved by me.

ELENA: You did. It was my sister.

MYLES: OK.

Beat. He carries on looking through the files. He then looks up again on a thought.

Wait…your sister's not epileptic?

ELENA: What? My sister? No.

MYLES: Then how could you have offended any epileptics with the phrase 'brain storm' if there were none in the room? Were there any in the room?

ELENA: No.

MYLES: Well then.

ELENA smiles.

What?

ELENA: Mr Brody, that question is exactly the reason you are my lawyer.

Beat. He finds his document.

MYLES: Here it is.

ELENA: This is what's happened to the world. Everyone gets offended about everything. A harmless phrase that you use without a thought. It's insanity.

MYLES: I was going through your statement last night.

ELENA: People picketing plays and television stations because the feel they have to attack something. It's not real, I don't buy it. I think they think they're supposed to be more offended than they are. They feel it's their duty. When what they're really feeling is hate. Hate is what binds a society together. The sooner people realise that the better.

What's dishonest is that it's dressed up as righteous indignation. As if to be offended makes the offended more pure. Well I'm offended by the news. I'm offended by war and greed and the profound stupidity of those in power, but I don't write in to the BBC and say you must stop all this reporting of rape and violence and corruption, it offends me.

MYLES: I wonder if we could get / back to…

ELENA: Yes, yes, sorry… (*She puts on her reading glasses.*) …you said there was an anomaly?

MYLES: …according to the officers who arrested you…

ELENA: …who completely ransacked my house and office…

MYLES: Yes, but…

ELENA: …took my laptop, my research documents, archival material from…

MYLES: My point is…

ELENA: Surely we can make a complaint.

MYLES: Not really.

ELENA: I'm still a citizen. They can't treat me like this. Like a common criminal.

MYLES: Section 29 H part 3 of the new bill says the police may use reasonable force if necessary.

ELENA: Reasonable force. Ridiculous.

MYLES: According to the arresting officer…

ELENA: Yes. I told him I was expecting them.

MYLES: … Yes. That's it.

ELENA: I was wondering how long it would take for you to get to that.

MYLES: You are aware, I mean I'm assuming you're aware that with this new law you could feasibly be looking at a seven year custodial sentence.

ELENA: I honestly didn't mean it to be provocative.

MYLES: If the court believes there was intent…that you knew what you were doing was criminal and yet persisted…

ELENA: Oh come on Myles, aren't you being just a little pedantic…

MYLES: This whole case relies on your character, on your veracity in court.

ELENA: I can do veracity.

MYLES: We'll have to flag it up at the preliminary hearing.

ELENA: There is no anomaly. I was aware of the new laws, absurd as they are, and expected them to be exercised. I didn't wilfully and cavalierly seek to flout them.

MYLES: In future be open and forthright.

ELENA: I've made a career out of being forthright.

MYLES: I'm serious. I can't defend you unless we absolutely trust each other.

Pause.

ELENA: This can't really be happening can it? I spent my whole life being controversial. I'm known for it. I've won awards for it. I've been on *Newsnight* for God's sake.

MYLES: The law changed.

ELENA: The law changed and now I'm here. What's this country come to? When you can't offend anyone by expressing an historical opinion?

MYLES: Offence isn't a crime in itself.

ELENA: There should never be an official version of history. A version that can't be questioned. Are we living in Stalinist Russia or Blairite Britain? Or are they the same thing?

MYLES: The Attorney General says he can prove you wilfully distorted historical evidence in order to present a version of events with the intention of stirring up racial hatred.

ELENA: Rubbish.

MYLES: As long as that wasn't your intention, we have a chance.

ELENA: My intention was to present the facts as I see them.

MYLES: As long as you can back up your theory with evidence.

ELENA: Historical interpretation isn't set in stone. It's a constant debate. A constant reassessment of events. Their significance and context are always in flux.

MYLES: That's a start, but…

ELENA: J S Mill said all truths need fundamental re-examination from time to time. Can you think of a better time than now to do that?

MYLES: The point is the new Racial and Religious Hatred Law asserts that you can't distort a truth to use against a particular group of people…

ELENA: New laws. That's all this government can do. Clearly if you want to eradicate something making it illegal is a sure-fire way of doing it. After all our prisons are empty. Nobody murders, nobody takes drugs. How about a new tax, a charge? A fiver for every offensive remark; with a discount if nobody hears you. We need to relearn how to think for ourselves in this country. Everybody's always telling you what to think, and then pretending your opinion's important. Like voting for who's the most odious person in a house on a reality TV show is thinking for yourself.

MYLES: I think the judge will expect us to be more specific than that.

ELENA: Free speech, real free speech, the right to say the hardest things, is the fuel in the fire of a free society. And if the strongest of us don't steel ourselves for the fight it'll be gone forever. Oh we censor ourselves all the time. Why? Out of fear? And then we – we rationalise the decision. We feel this or that about a group, and then ask ourselves: 'Am I wrong to feel that way?' As though what we feel is somehow primitive, as though our deepest human instincts aren't to be trusted. There's this piffle being put about by the chattering liberalistas that if we respect each other's taboos there'll be some kind of cultural harmony. When actually what'll happen is that there'll be a massive explosion. If the people are muzzled, one day, mark my words, one day they'll hit boiling point and the gag will fly off and there'll be an almighty scream.

Beat.

MYLES: I have some sympathy with that argument, I do, but it doesn't change the fact that we have to prove that, based on the evidence, you came to a reasonable conclusion. That your ideas have nothing to do with racism.

Pause. There is a new energy between them as MYLES fixes ELENA with an almost challenging stare.

ELENA: Seven years?

MYLES: Yes.

ELENA: Just for publishing a hundred-page book.

MYLES: It's my job to see it doesn't come to that.

ELENA: Then you'd better be bloody good at your job.

MYLES: I am.

Pause.

ELENA: You remind me of someone.

MYLES: I do?

ELENA: An old boyfriend from Cambridge days. A biologist. I used to call him my iceberg.

MYLES: He didn't sink a big / ship...

ELENA: No. Lot going on underneath.

MYLES: Right.

ELENA: He became very successful, very young. Got that success that makes people zealous about themselves. They stop growing. Yes you're very like him. He was also... blank.

Pause.

MYLES: I'm done for today.

ELENA: Would you get a couple of things for me? I'm running out of inhaler. For my asthma.

MYLES: I'll make a note.

MYLES scribbles it down on his papers.

ELENA: Thank you. They won't let me out even to the shops.

MYLES: You said a couple of things.

ELENA: Yes.

MYLES: What else?

ELENA: Twenty Benson and Hedges.

Blackout.

SCENE THREE

Flat. The next morning.

There are empty glasses and bottles strewn about from the night before. The shower is heard coming from the bathroom, loudly. TARA enters in whatever she wears for bed. She stretches and yawns. She's had a frantic night and it tells in her appearance. She picks up the empty bottle and goes off to the kitchen.

The shower continues. MYLES rushes in. He is late for work. He is dressed in a pair of boxers and a T-shirt with a towel over his shoulder. He tries to get into the bathroom but it is locked. The shower is running. He waits. Then bangs on the door.

MYLES: Tara! Come on. It's nearly eight! I have to get to work.

He bangs more, but to no avail. Then he gives up. Casually he picks up the remote for the TV and flicks it on. He drifts idly through the channels, then settles on one, entranced.

TARA re-enters from the kitchen. She almost creeps on behind him and peers over his shoulder to see what he is watching. MYLES spins round.

Oh.

He switches the TV off.

MYLES: I thought you were in the shower.

TARA: Boyfriend. I didn't know you were into *Big Brother*.

MYLES: I'm not. Into it? What?

TARA: Fine.

31

MYLES: I'm not 'into' it.

TARA: Fine.

MYLES: I was just flicking.

TARA: Who do you think's going to win?

MYLES: I don't know their names. I told you, I was just idly passing the time.

Beat. They wait and hear the shower.

TARA: I think Nikki's going to win.

MYLES: What? No way. Nikki? She's off her box. It'll be the one with the thing.

TARA: I knew you were into it.

MYLES: (*Looking at his watch.*) What's he doing in there for Christ's sake?

TARA: Bungee jumping?

MYLES: No, I mean, why is he taking so long?

TARA: He's very fanatical about his showers.

MYLES: Fanatical? Is he washing every muscle individually?

TARA: Please don't be rude about my boyfriend.

MYLES: A bloke who spends that amount of time salivating marvellously over his gym-tastic body…

TARA: He's not gay. He's not gay. Trust me.

MYLES: Granted he compulsively feels he has to publicly fondle and smooch and generally climb all over you at every available / opportunity.

TARA: Yeah could you not audibly growl when we're cuddling up on the couch? You can be heard.

MYLES: So don't do it in front of me. Yeah? Go to your room, can't you go to your room?

32

TARA: You go to yours.

MYLES: And could you please tell him that not everyone in this flat is enthralled by his baby-talking and, I'm sorry, but very unfunny jokes. Did he write for Cannon and Ball in a former life or what?

TARA: Actually he's very funny.

MYLES: That's a lie and you know it.

TARA: I mean I know you're a little bit jealous, but there's no need to be catty…

MYLES: Oh please. Please. Jealous? Please.

TARA: No I think you do, you feel a tiny bit emasculated by his size…

MYLES: I think making up those dumb letters for the *Mirror*'s made you see things in a very / distorted…

TARA: That's right, I've seen the way you shake his hand. I've seen the searing pain in your face as he grips your hand. Your eyes water and you do that crazed grin.

MYLES: I'm being polite.

TARA: You wouldn't know 'being polite' if it smashed your kneecaps.

MYLES: Well maybe if you didn't leave bits of yourself in every possible crevice…

TARA: Bits of myself!?

MYLES: You're very messy actually.

TARA: Are you making a complaint?

MYLES: Well look at this place.

TARA: Did you try phoning Housekeeping?

MYLES: …half-eaten yoghurt tubs and flip-flops left in the most annoying places. It's no wonder I'm grumpy.

TARA: You were born that way, I know / your type.

MYLES: …your…your…you know, those pathetically bereft-looking rolled up socks everywhere. In the living room, in the bathroom, I found one in the cutlery drawer.

TARA: Well you're not so tidy, with all your files strewn all over the flat.

MYLES: And some of those socks are mauve. I told you I don't like the colour mauve, that it upsets me. Are you doing it deliberately? / Are you?

TARA: It's all you ever do. Work. You never speak to me when you come in. You totally ignore me.

MYLES: Oh I'm sorry, I must have drifted off, did we get married?

Pause. TARA stares at MYLES.

God he really is fanatical about this shower.

TARA: He told me he goes into a sort of trance.

MYLES: Trance?

TARA: I think it's nice. Deep.

MYLES: Oh for God's sake I can't…I can't wait. I'll have to do without.

MYLES stomps off.

TARA: (*Shouting off after him.*) You'd be lucky to marry me! (*No reply. She presses on regardless.*) I'm fantastic. I'm witty and clever, and nice, but you wouldn't know any of that would you because you only ever speak to me when you absolutely have to. Which, by the way, is usually to complain.

MYLES returns, now with a shirt on and doing up his tie.

MYLES: (*As he enters.*) I wouldn't have to if I wasn't kept up all night by you two fff… (*Stops.*)

MYLES looks at her, realises he's about to cross a line.

TARA: What?

MYLES: Forget it.

MYLES carries on dressing.

TARA: (*Horrified at the realisation.*) Do we keep you up with our fucking?

MYLES: (*Pause as he considers what to say.*) Sometimes.

MYLES goes off again.

TARA: How embarrassing. That's not good.

MYLES comes back with his trousers and puts them on.

MYLES: He's taking an extraordinarily long time in that shower.

TARA: You can hear us?

MYLES: Seriously I think he's slipped from a trance to a coma.

TARA: Are we very loud? I don't…I mean I'm not really lucid during fucking.

MYLES: I mean you're extremely…you know…vocal. It's a sort of shrieking thing you do. I can see ripples in my cocoa.

MYLES goes off. The shower continues. TARA thinks. MYLES returns with his jacket and briefcase.

TARA: Do you think he's drowned in there?

MYLES: Just make sure the body's removed by the time I get home.

TARA: You're going?

MYLES: I'll clean my teeth at the office.

TARA: I mean.

MYLES: What? You're always starting sentences that never lead anywhere. What is it?

TARA: I'm just trying to…you know…

MYLES: I haven't got time for this.

TARA: You never have.

MYLES: And make sure the place isn't a tip as usual.

MYLES leaves. TARA shouts after him.

TARA: I'll make sure there's a little chocolate on your pillow as well shall I? Bastard.

Beat. TARA suddenly bangs on the bathroom door.

(*Furious.*) What the fuck are you doing in there? Come on!

SCENE FOUR

Safe-house. Study. Later that day.

MYLES is itchy and fidgety and grouchy because he hasn't had his shower. ELENA has a jigsaw puzzle in the first stages of completion on the table in front of her – it is clearly a very large and complicated one and it distracts her throughout the scene.

MYLES: In your book you suggest that the gas chambers were a fiction created by the Jews after the war.

ELENA: (*After a deliberate pause.*) I didn't get my things.

MYLES: What?

ELENA: I asked you for a ventalin cartridge.

MYLES: Yes. I was going to get them this morning. I was running late.

ELENA: And some cigarettes. I didn't sleep well.

MYLES: I'm sorry, the asthma? You needed your inhaler.

ELENA: No, I needed a cigarette. But as it happens I found this jigsaw puzzle. It was very restful.

MYLES: Anyway...

ELENA: I haven't completed it yet but I think it's a Klimt. It's surprisingly diverting.

MYLES: As I was saying...

ELENA: You don't mind if I tinker with it during our sessions, it has me in its grip?

MYLES: Your book posits that the gas chambers were a fiction created by the Jews.

ELENA: (*Searching for the place for the jigsaw piece she holds in her hand.*) Yes.

MYLES: You allege – this is in order to squeeze money from the Allies and to garner sympathy from the international community.

ELENA: Well, that's a theory for why they would...

MYLES: Right. And you assert this theory?

ELENA: How else would they acquire their state?

MYLES: Israel?

ELENA: I don't blame them, statehood's a messy business. America slaughtered the native population. Australia the Aborigines. Every major modern power has their original sin. Israel has the myth of the holocaust.

MYLES: See this...this is exactly the kind of racist ideology the prosecution will suggest compromises your work and spreads hatred.

ELENA: I'm simply saying that countries are born in blood. That they're taken by all means available. The Jews are nothing if not historically aware and politically acute.

They knew that European guilt would buy them billions in hand-outs…ninety billion marks from Germany, all the fire-power they could get their hands on from America…

MYLES: But this is my point. If the prosecution can prove that you're anti-Semitic…that you're stirring up anti-Jewish feeling by suggesting they manipulated and lied, a terrible, unthinkable thing to lie about for their own gain…

ELENA: If it's anti-Semitic to speak the truth.

MYLES: Let's start from – (*He starts going through his papers, they are in a mess.*) Talk about…uh…talk about the – sorry – you talk about in your papers the different schools of historical…

ELENA: Yes.

MYLES: I wonder if you could…

ELENA: It's quite simple there are two major schools in historical thinking when it comes to the legend of the final solution.

MYLES: Yes. The… (*Searches for some documents, but he's all fingers and thumbs.*) …sorry, I remember this from my reading.

ELENA: Well…the Intentionalists say Hitler came to power intending all along to murder Jews, while the Functionalists argue that the final solution was arrived at incrementally. That Hitler just wanted to rid Germany of them, send them to Madagascar, but that when that became untenable they started knocking them off.

MYLES: All right and you reject both of these theories?

ELENA: Revisionists believe that the camps were meant for labour at the I G Farben munitions factory. Slavery, yes, but not genocide. They were a valuable and cheap workforce. It made no sense for the Germans, who were fighting a world war, to annihilate them.

MYLES: Right. Yes.

ELENA: I mean, I suppose, angry their labour had not been sufficiently remunerated, there was this gang of imaginative Jews who started coming up with the notion of gas chambers.

MYLES: Yes, well if we go to trial, don't expand on a theme unless directed to.

ELENA: I'm just trying to answer the question as fully as possible Myles.

MYLES: Just remember the prosecuting counsel is going to be looking for the chink in your armour, so the less you show the better.

ELENA: But I don't want him twisting my words.

MYLES: Then the less words you give him to twist the better.

ELENA: Is that why you're so reticent? You don't want to give people too much to twist.

MYLES: This isn't about me.

ELENA: That's what you lawyers do isn't it? Why if this goes to trial some clever lawyer will make my interpretations look like sinister malfeasance, aimed at provoking anti-Jewish hatred. And you don't seem as though you're on top of this. If you can't help me get the truth out there.

MYLES: Look, Elena…

ELENA: Because this is what this is about. Even if I have to pay with my freedom, the truth must come out.

MYLES: But on the day the opposing barrister will be on top of his game. He'll be in your face like a bull terrier. He won't stop until he's dismantled your argument and your career and your character.

ELENA: Bring it on I say. Let me have my day. Let them wheel out historian after historian to attack my writing, I'll strike them down. All of them.

MYLES: This isn't men's tennis. There's a dialectic. You don't just whack in your big serve and run away. You got to have the shots to back it up.

ELENA: I've got the shots.

MYLES: Really? Even when confronted with the irrefutable fact that before 1941 there were a considerably larger number of Jews than after 1945?

ELENA: Yes.

MYLES: What would one say to that?

ELENA: I never said Jews didn't die during World War Two.

MYLES: Yes, but…

ELENA: Many did. Millions of people died. Twenty million Russians. It was the most devastating war in history. Of course they died.

MYLES: OK, but…

ELENA: I'm not a monster Myles. I never denied there was a holocaust. You won't find that anywhere in my writing. I know about the Nuremberg laws, about the Lateran Council ordering Jews to be segregated from gentiles, to wear badges, to be forced to live in Ghettos. But isn't that what they've wanted all along? Don't we see this with ethnic groups all the time? Living in Ghettos. Wearing markings denoting their origins. Marrying within their own culture. It's what they want.

MYLES: Actually in my reading it seems clear the Jews of 1930s Germany were the most assimilated of any ethnic group in history. One in two were marrying out. So they were trying to integrate.

ELENA: Yes to slip into the machinery of power undetected.

MYLES: Oh please.

ELENA: In this country too. It was the great Jewish media moguls who brought down the peacemaker Neville Chamberlain, and appointed Churchill. Churchill. That pug faced warmonger, that fascist.

MYLES: Churchill was a fascist now was he?

ELENA: He was a drunken, bald, silly-voiced corrupt puppet of the Jewish cabal that ruled the roost and still does.

MYLES: If the Jewish cabal 'ruled the roost', as you say, why didn't the RAF bomb the train tracks leading to Auschwitz that would have stopped the killing machine?

ELENA: Because Churchill didn't want to give away to the Germans that Bletchley Park had cracked their Enigma codes.

MYLES: Right. Yes I remember reading that…

ELENA: Remember Myles this is my topic. I've been studying this subject my whole career. My books and documentaries have been widely praised.

MYLES: I know, I've seen, I've seen you on TV, we all have. We've all had to listen to it.

ELENA: Well I'm sorry if I didn't entertain you.

MYLES: Oh I found it very entertaining, trust me.

ELENA: My God Myles, don't get all emotional about it. Anyone would think you were Jewish yourself.

Stop. MYLES looks at her.

MYLES: I apologise. I didn't sleep well last night. It won't happen again.

ELENA: You're not…are you?

MYLES: Getting back to your book.

ELENA: You didn't answer my question.

MYLES: We really are pressed for time.

ELENA: It's a simple yes or no Myles.

MYLES: Would it make a difference?

ELENA: To whom?

MYLES: No. I'm not. I'm not Jewish. OK? Can we proceed?

ELENA: Of course.

MYLES, now even more agitated flicks sharply through the documents.

You seem agitated. Not yourself. Why didn't you sleep?

MYLES: …it's nothing.

ELENA: Well it's not nothing. It's affecting me directly. Come on.

MYLES: I moved to a new flat. I'm sharing.

ELENA: Oh.

MYLES: There was someone comatose in the shower this morning.

ELENA: Comatose…

MYLES: It's really not relevant.

ELENA: It's hard to share with selfish people.

MYLES: Well I wouldn't call her selfish…

ELENA: Her?

MYLES: It was her boyfriend.

ELENA: Oh. Her boyfriend was in the shower?

MYLES: Yes. Can we…

ELENA: And she's being territorial is she?

MYLES: No.

ELENA: Yes. I know the type. Vain and stupid and flaunting her preening, obsessive compulsive boyfriend about the place so as to make you feel inadequate.

MYLES: Actually she's not like that at all.

ELENA: Just as you wish.

Pause.

MYLES: OK. Let's talk specifically about gas chambers.

ELENA: Very well.

MYLES: In your book, you refer to the Leuchter Report.

ELENA: Yes.

MYLES: Tell me about this report.

ELENA: Fred Leuchter scientifically demonstrates that the gas Zyklon B could not have been used to kill people in the camps.

MYLES: But the report admits that traces of hydrocyanic acid, the chemical released by Zyklon B, were found in the walls of certain rooms at Auschwitz.

ELENA: These were delousing rooms. Hydrocyanic acid is a powerful insecticide. The clothes of the inmates were deloused. There are photos, in my book, there are photos of these chambers.

MYLES: Yes.

ELENA: Look at them.

MYLES: Yes.

ELENA: If hundreds of people were being gassed to death, wouldn't they have tried to escape?

MYLES: What's your point?

ELENA: Look at the doors. There's no way those flimsy things could withstand the force of a hoard of people fighting for their lives. Look. You must agree.

MYLES: Yes.

ELENA: Good. You see. There's room for doubt. That's all I'm saying. Doubt, not denial. Questioning. Exploration. Doubt what you're told.

MYLES: Go on.

ELENA: Yes. Thank you. Thank you. You'll let me talk to you. We'll understand each other.

MYLES: You were talking about delousing rooms.

ELENA: Yes.

MYLES: But no one disputes delousing rooms existed.

ELENA: No. Just that another room was set aside for mass extermination. The point is more traces of the chemical compound were found in the delousing rooms, the rooms all historians agree were used for delousing. Far more. So this other room could not have been used for gassing people because they'd have found more traces there, surely.

MYLES: So you're saying there was no other room?

ELENA: Yes. I'm saying there was no other room.

MYLES: OK.

ELENA: And for that they want to put me in prison. Because I go against the tide. Because I don't subscribe to the general view. But this is my job Myles...

MYLES: Yes.

ELENA: I'm a historian. I'm meant to ask these questions. I'm meant to reassess. Re-evaluate. It's how I get to the... Look...I don't expect you to agree with me on my interpretation of history, but I do expect you to appreciate

THE GLASS ROOM: ACT ONE

my right to interpret it how I can. If I'm wrong, then I'm wrong. We once believed the world was flat. People were deemed heretics. Lunatics. They were imprisoned.

MYLES: Yes. That won't wash with the trial judge.

ELENA: But isn't it dangerous to execute history or astronomy or anything else by general consensus? The world can't move forward unless original thinkers come along and asks questions, hard questions about our received wisdom. Challenging the mainstream. Putting their reputations and even their lives on the line.

MYLES: As you are?

ELENA: Yes. As I am.

MYLES: So you admit your views are not widely accepted.

ELENA: Well...insofar as...

MYLES: Insofar as most people don't agree with you.

ELENA: Free speech isn't saying whatever you like as long as everyone agrees with you. Answer this question Myles. Do you think Muslim women should be allowed to wear the veil?

MYLES: Yes. Of course. Tolerance means tolerance for all, not just those we like the look of...

ELENA: In a recent survey it was found that ninety-eight per cent of people in this country disagree with you. You're in such a small minority by your standards you're almost insane.

MYLES: Yes but you do have a duty as an academic professor to support your opinion with facts. With hard evidence.

ELENA: We'll get to that. Admit to me that you think I have a point. Come on. Admit that there is a germ of doubt in your mind that all the things they've told you, the media, Hollywood, all the things you thought about this subject...

there might be some room for questioning. That's all I ask. If we can prove that, we'll win. Surely.

SCENE FIVE

Flat. That night.

MYLES comes in. He's had a very long day and he sighs deeply. He holds a briefcase. He notices a bottle of white wine on the coffee table with a yellow Post-it note stuck to the neck. He rips off the note and reads it. He smiles to himself, then puts down his case and goes to his stereo and turns it on. It is Arvo Part's Third Symphony. Then he goes off to the kitchen to get a corkscrew. He comes back with the wine open and a glass. He pours the wine and steels himself and then drinks it down in one go. It is far too good. Something he hasn't done for a while. Then he pours another, savouring it this time. He looks around the house and enjoys the emptiness.

He then takes his briefcase and opens it, taking out a large file. He sits at the coffee table and begins some serious work.

Silence.

Suddenly TARA bursts into the room. She is dressed very sexily and smartly, for a night out, but the make-up on her face is smudged as if she's been crying.

TARA: (*Melodramatic.*) Hello.

> *MYLES grunts.*

> How's it going?

> *She stares at MYLES, who does this whole exchange with his head in documents.*

MYLES: I had a terrible day.

TARA: (*Choked.*) That's a shame.

MYLES: I got your note. How was dinner?

TARA: Edible.

MYLES: I opened the wine. Thanks.

TARA: Like it?

MYLES: Quaffable.

TARA: I'm so pleased.

MYLES: Have a glass.

> *TARA grabs the wine and sucks it from the bottle. MYLES does not look up. TARA slams the bottle down on the table.*

TARA: Sorry about keeping you up last night.

MYLES: Forget it. As long as I can really get on top of it tonight...

TARA: OK. Well I'll leave you to it then.

MYLES: Thanks.

TARA: I'm just going to lock myself in my room and weep.

MYLES: (*Not looking up.*) Night then.

> *TARA is aggravated. She stands there and forces herself to sob audibly. MYLES's head moves ever so slightly. Then he thinks better of it and gets back to work.*

> *TARA is beside herself. She goes to the stereo and switches off the music. MYLES still doesn't look up. TARA puts on 'Winner Takes It All' by Abba. MYLES now looks up.*

I get it. I get it. Turn it off. For Christ's sake turn it off!

> *TARA turns the music off.*

TARA: Men are slime. They're the scab on the worm that none of the other worms want to be friends with.

MYLES: Chunky?

TARA: That coward.

MYLES: I'll make you a coffee.

TARA: I don't want coffee. I want revenge. I want his dick on a stick. I want…I want… Oh I want…

MYLES: Look…

TARA: I want…a life.

MYLES: Wait there.

TARA: I said forget the coffee. Men are so hopeless. Don't you understand? I just want to yell at someone.

MYLES: Yeah but I just…

TARA: Stay exactly where you are if you value your testicles.

MYLES: OK.

TARA: He said… Get this: he said…he's scared of me.

MYLES: Well…

TARA: Said I was too full-on for him. That I was always talking about love and forever and what I'd do to him if he disappointed me.

MYLES: Well…

TARA: He told me he was frightened. That at night if we've had a disagreement he sometimes can't get to sleep because he doesn't know what I might do to him. I found him in bed once clutching his ball-sack, his jaw clenched. That's a brink from which there is no return my friend let me tell you.

MYLES: Then perhaps it's, you know, for the best and stuff.

TARA: (*Beat. Then slow and sinister and full of contempt.*) Oh my God you really are utterly, utterly useless. What a tired, trite piece of crap to trot out.

MYLES: I was only trying to help.

TARA: Yeah? Fat lot of help that is!

MYLES: You're drunk. At least I hope you are, otherwise you're being incredibly rude.

TARA: Oh am I? Well you're being incredibly...bland!

MYLES: I'm making you that coffee like it or not.

TARA: Are you taking charge?

MYLES: Yes. That's exactly what I'm doing. I'm taking charge.

TARA smiles. MYLES goes. TARA looks at his case and is very intrigued.

TARA: (*Talks loudly.*) Anyway over dinner tonight I was telling him how I had ambitions, you know, to do something in journalism, proper journalism, to write about something important, and he goes, 'Don't you need an education for that?' And I say I've got an education. And he goes, 'Yeah not a Mickey Mouse History of Art degree.' And he goes, 'Yeah OK, probably need something to fall back on when your looks go.' Huh? What about that one? That's one for the books.

MYLES re-enters.

MYLES: There's no coffee. I put some tea on.

TARA: So then I get the squeezy ketchup bottle that's on the table, you know amidst all the other condiments and I squeeze it all over his white Valentino shirt. Anyway it was just after that he told me he wasn't completely happy in the relationship.

MYLES is looking at her. Finally TARA notices.

What?

MYLES: What?

TARA: You...

MYLES: No. Nothing. I...

TARA: Myles...

49

MYLES: Just…

TARA: Yes?

MYLES: Yes. No. Great. Forget it. I'll check on the tea.

MYLES goes.

TARA: (*Sighs. Talks loud.*) I'm drawn to these beautiful bastards. I can't help it. I can't leave them alone. I know they'll hurt me, I know it's bad for me. And this guy votes Tory as well. That should have been a heads-up.

She drinks from the wine and flicks idly, if cheekily, through the file that MYLES has been working on. As she reads she starts to sober up. It catches her eye. She is breathless. She sits down to read, amazed and perhaps a little appalled. MYLES re-enters.

MYLES: What are you doing?

TARA: I…

MYLES: That's confidential.

TARA: I wasn't thinking. I'm sorry.

MYLES: Jesus did you…

TARA: I didn't…I'm really sorry.

MYLES: Did you see?

TARA: I didn't mean to look, I don't know what came over me…

MYLES: Tara. Did you see?

Pause.

TARA: Yes. I'm sorry.

MYLES: Shit.

TARA: It's not my business.

MYLES: No. It's not.

TARA: I'll just pretend I didn't see it.

MYLES: You think you can do that? Just forget it?

Beat.

TARA: No. Probably not.

Pause.

MYLES: The tea.

MYLES goes off.

TARA: Shit. Shit shit shit.

TARA sits her head in her hands. MYLES returns with a mug.

Thanks.

TARA drinks.

MYLES: Tara you really can't tell anyone about what you saw just now.

TARA: I understand.

Silence. TARA drinks. MYLES checks his papers.

MYLES: I have to ask you a question?

TARA: OK.

MYLES: It's important that you answer me honestly.

TARA: What is it?

MYLES: Did you see the address?

TARA: Address?

MYLES: Of the safe-house.

TARA: No. She's in a safe-house?

MYLES: This is extremely important.

TARA: I swear, I didn't see it.

Pause.

What's she like?

MYLES: Well…

TARA: Is she scary? I bet she's a right mentalist?

MYLES: She's eccentric.

TARA: Is she inspiring?

MYLES: Given the right circumstances. If she kept her head.

TARA: How terrifying.

MYLES: Yes but only if you gag her. If you let her talk, her arguments will eventually unravel. Give her enough rope, she'll hang herself.

TARA: Arguments? Isn't she just a big fat racist?

MYLES: Well yes, her rhetoric's full of bile, full of half-truths, prejudice, fallacies, distortions, but just because she's wrong, doesn't mean we should silence her. Just making people ask, 'What does she know that's so dangerous and exciting we're not allowed to hear it?' Look. People get tired of talking long before they get tired of fighting. Talking is hard. And it's talking to the people we fundamentally disconnect with which will give us any hope of a future. With the people we love we can sit in silence, but with the people who hate us, we have no other choice. We have to talk.

TARA: Yes but don't you feel…conflicted? Sitting with a woman like that every day? Defending a woman like that?

MYLES: Conflicted?

TARA: I thought you were Jewish. Doesn't it make you feel a bit shit?

MYLES: I'm not really a bona fide Jew. The rule is your Mum has to be Jewish. My Mum's a Catholic from Belfast.

TARA: A Catholic Jew. You should feel doubly guilty.

MYLES: Actually I don't feel anything at all.

TARA: I'm sorry to hear that.

MYLES: My Dad always tried to get me into the whole Jewish heritage thing, bought me these books, but it's all death and pogroms and running away at a moment's notice.

TARA: Running away. Hey that's something you're good at.

MYLES: Excuse me?

TARA: No it's just – that's the first time you've talked to me like that. The first time you've opened up.

MYLES: Tara…

TARA: I feel I only know a tiny fraction of you, even though I see you every day. Every morning and every night for four months. Even though I know what you look like asleep.

MYLES: You've seen me asleep?

TARA: On the couch.

MYLES: Oh. Look…

TARA: It's OK I like it when you talk. Talk some more. Stay up with me.

MYLES: I shouldn't. I have to face her tomorrow. I have to be ready. There's so much I don't know. A lifetime's work… I really need to be on top of my game.

TARA: Yeah. Of course. It's late anyway, I should go to bed. Night then.

MYLES: Night.

TARA goes.

MYLES watches the space left by her exit.

SCENE SIX

Safe-house. Study. The next morning.

MYLES enters with a carrier bag.

ELENA: He's back. With a bag.

MYLES: Your inhaler.

ELENA: Ready to go into battle?

MYLES: Battle?

ELENA: I hope you've done your homework I'm feeling sharp today. (*Takes the cigarette packet out of the bag and rips it open.*) Aah, Benson and Hedges my dearest friends. How did you get them past Marjoram? Or Cerberus as I affectionately call her.

MYLES: Waited for Potts to take over. They swap every half an hour.

ELENA: You know they watch us.

MYLES: There are no cameras in here.

ELENA: There. (*She stares out as if looking in the large mirror.*) Scrutinising my every remark.

MYLES: I assure you everything we say in this room is confidential.

ELENA: I've been staring at that mirror.

MYLES looks at the mirror. Out to the auditorium.

I'm sure I can see shadows behind it...moving about. I'm sure it's one of those two-way mirrors.

MYLES: Do you think you should be smoking?

ELENA: Let them watch. Good. Let them see. Let them hear. What? Reason? Justice?

MYLES: I mean what with your asthma.

ELENA: I like to face down the demon. Laugh in the face of...whatever...tackle terror head on. I've always swam against the tide. I've always felt an affiliation with the underdog. My father was an American. He was in the communist party in the fifties and was hounded out of his native country by Senator McCarthy's witch-hunts.

MYLES: I know.

ELENA: I once knew a boy who was born with no fingers. They were short stubs...sort of chopped off half way. He was mercilessly bullied. His parents came up with all kinds of creative career ideas, but there was only one thing he was determined to do in life.

MYLES: Play the violin?

ELENA: Yes!

MYLES: I was joking.

ELENA: Well the piano. He was a pianist. The really rangy stuff was difficult, the Rach Three was out the window, but he had a great tone. I like to think I would have been like that.

MYLES: Stubborn?

ELENA: Indefatigable. Fearless.

MYLES: I hate to point it out but smoking with asthma is not the same as heroically overcoming a deformity...

ELENA: Hadn't we better get on with my preparation?

MYLES: It's more kamikaze, than heroic.

ELENA: You know I get death threats. But do I let it stop me? Stop the work I've been dedicated to my whole career? My staff too. My son. My translator in Hungary received a dead rat in his mail. It had been gassed. You'd better be vigilant you could be on their list.

MYLES: Me?

ELENA: Are we here to talk about my health or this case?

MYLES: Fine.

MYLES drops a file in front of ELENA. She looks at it.

ELENA: What's that?

MYLES: The prosecution sent it.

ELENA looks at the document.

ELENA: Ah yes that.

MYLES: The Munich Institute for Contemporary History.

ELENA: Piffle.

MYLES: Well this piffle is universally hailed as the most prestigious source in Germany regarding Nazi crimes during World War Two.

ELENA: I read it.

MYLES: OK, so you know it states quite clearly that there were thirteen camps where gassing took place.

ELENA: Mainly Treblinka and Auschwitz. Yes.

MYLES: Just to take Auschwitz. The extermination camp in Birkenau – a sort of annex of Auschwitz – was established in the autumn of 1941. By the end of November 1944, the report states, more than a million Jews and at least four thousand gypsies had been murdered in the nine chambers by the gas Zyklon B.

ELENA: So it says.

He drops another file in front of her.

MYLES: Here's another document you may not have seen.

ELENA looks at it.

A village called Bad Arolsen had been storing a vast trove of Nazi files.

ELENA: Yes.

MYLES: A couple of days ago the German Justice Minister
ordered they be released. In them the details of medical
experiments, names of collaborators on the Lebensborn
programme.

ELENA: As it happens I have read these documents.

MYLES: You have?

ELENA: I was given access by… Well you don't need to know
who… Let's just say…a friend.

MYLES: Quite.

ELENA: The point is in the thirty million papers stored there,
there is no record at all of the Jews allegedly gassed at
Auschwitz.

MYLES: No.

ELENA: Thirty million documents Myles.

MYLES: Yes.

ELENA: Wouldn't you have thought there would be some
mention of them. If there were as many as you say.

MYLES: As I say? Not I. The Munich Institute for
Contemporary History. Every major historian on the
subject. Hundreds of eyewitnesses who survived the
camps.

ELENA: Yes and don't we know it. They're always at it aren't
they? Poor us. Look what happened to us. It's a racket.
And their number keeps swelling.

MYLES: God. Sorry. 'Their number keeps swelling'? Wait.
Yesterday you said it's the same old gang. The same small
coterie of people who keep testifying to the gas chambers.
Now it's 'their number keeps swelling'. I don't think your
contradictions will stand up to forensic examination in the
witness box.

ELENA: What about the case of Paul Rassinier? This was a socialist parliamentary deputy, a political prisoner of the Nazis. He was interned in a concentration camp and claims he never saw a gas chamber. An eyewitness. A survivor.

MYLES: I'll come to eyewitness statements in due course.

ELENA: I ask again. Where is the evidence in the Bad Arolsen records of these so-called victims of gassing?

MYLES: Most of the people gassed at Birkenau were done so on arrival and so no records were taken of them.

ELENA: Very neat. But no record is no proof of anything. And the burden of proof is on the accuser.

MYLES: OK. Talk to me about proof. Go through your arguments again.

ELENA: Yes. I will. Clearly and concisely. Without emotion. Facts.

MYLES: Fine.

ELENA: So we've said about the doors. And the traces of compound.

MYLES: Yes.

ELENA: You mentioned the rooms used for gassing at Birkenau. You will see from the plans of the camp that these rooms were in close proximity to the ovens.

MYLES: Yes.

ELENA: It's argued that Zyklon B pellets were dropped into these rooms.

MYLES: It is.

ELENA: But Zyklon B is a very explosive gas. If that was the case, and being so close to the furnaces, the whole place would have gone up like a Catherine Wheel.

MYLES: Go on.

ELENA: OK but let's say they did manage to use these pellets. That there were buildings for extermination far enough away from the ovens. It takes approximately twenty hours to air a room which is disinfected with Zyklon B. Yet all these so-called eyewitness accounts consistently give a time of twenty to thirty minutes from when the gassing started to when the bodies were carried out.

MYLES: True.

ELENA: Impossible. That would mean that the Sonderkommando, the people carrying out the bodies, would have suffocated to death too. And they didn't. And even if they were masked up or whatever, why weren't they killed by the Nazis when they saw the end coming?

MYLES: Well they were. Most of them. Those were their orders. The Nazi leadership took great care to obliterate all traces of the death camps. Orders had been given to destroy all gas chambers and that no survivor of the camps was to fall into the hands of the Allies.

ELENA: Unlike the Nazis to be so slipshod as to let so many slip through the net.

MYLES: It's true some Sonderkommando did survive.

ELENA: Good for them. Further, these rooms were far too small to have the capacity to gas the millions of people as claimed in these spurious documents from the Institute of Contemporary History in Munich. The chambers were about two hundred and ten square metres. Not vast slaughter rooms. But even if they were working round the clock as is claimed, the gas chambers – here – I'll show you: look at these photographs of the remnants of Krema One.

ELENA shows MYLES a photo in her book.

These rooms were never sealed. Now wouldn't you seal a room if you wanted to kill everyone inside with gas pellets and keep safe the people outside? The engineers dropping in the pellets? The guards? The Sonderkommando?

MYLES: I suppose so.

ELENA: Finally there was no talk anywhere in the Wannsee Conference, or in *Mein Kampf*, or the ecumenical councils, or anywhere about the use of gas against the Jews. In fact Hitler had first-hand experience of it. He was gassed during the first war, and he knew it to be ineffective. Hitler didn't want to exterminate the Jews. He wanted to use them to build a greater Germany. He had ambition.

MYLES: Stick to the facts.

ELENA: These are the facts. Hitler cared about his fellow man. As he recovered from the gassing he said: 'Poor miserable fellow, will you start howling when there are thousands whose lot is a hundred times worse than yours.' These are the words of a humanitarian.

Pause. MYLES opens the folder.

MYLES: OK. Let's take it bit by bit.

ELENA: Yes.

MYLES: First you say the doors were not strong enough to have held in a large group of people, who would necessarily be trying to escape.

MYLES opens his file.

ELENA: That's correct. Again, there's no physical evidence. None of the Kremas remain today in their original state. They were destroyed at the end of the war as the Soviet army approached.

MYLES: So there's no physical evidence to show how the doors actually looked.

ELENA: No.

MYLES: If they were going to hold in this group of people fighting for their lives, these doors would have to be massive, wouldn't they?

ELENA: Absolutely.

MYLES: Possibly reinforced with iron bars. Perhaps with a small peephole protected from the inside by a strong metal grid, so the victims could not break the glass?

ELENA: Probably.

MYLES: Very much like this door.

He drops a photograph in front of her.

ELENA: What's this?

MYLES: A door found on the grounds of the camp.

ELENA: It doesn't convince me. It could have been from anywhere.

MYLES: But it is empirical evidence that such a door existed. Next you claim that the rooms were actually used as delousing chambers.

ELENA: Zyklon B is an insecticide. It releases HCN…

MYLES: And it's that chemical that causes death.

ELENA: To lice.

MYLES: But HCN is far more effective on warm blooded animals according to all the scientific experts. So the period of exposure to HCN is far longer for delousing clothes than that needed for killing people. Which would explain why fewer traces of the compound were found in the extermination chambers than the delousing chambers as you rightly point out.

ELENA: Well…

He picks up another document.

MYLES: This is the Merck Index.

ELENA: What about it?

MYLES: It's a manual dealing with toxicity and flammability of chemicals.

ELENA: And?

MYLES: On insects, a concentration of sixteen parts per million is used with exposure of seventy-two hours. On humans three hundred parts per million is needed. And will kill them in fifteen minutes. A swift enough death to allow, working round the clock, a lot of killing sessions a day. Enough to pack in all the new arrivals and exterminate a lot of people, wouldn't you say? Over four years...a million?

ELENA: I'm not a mathematician.

MYLES: Quite. Next. You said that the furnaces were situated close to the extermination rooms and that using a potent gas like Zyklon B would have caused a massive explosion.

ELENA: Yes. Yes. What about that?

MYLES: Again, according to the manual, the concentration of HCN necessary to cause death is nearly two hundred times lower than that necessary to cause an explosion.

ELENA: Well you've certainly done your homework.

MYLES: Entry 4688.

ELENA looks.

Remember it takes three hundred parts per million to kill a human. But it takes fifty-six thousand to cause an explosion. So. No Catherine Wheel.

ELENA: What about the twenty hours it takes to clear the room.

MYLES: Well it would if the rooms were not forcibly ventilated.

ELENA: Which they weren't.

MYLES: Well. As we said before, the SS dynamited all the extermination chambers before they abandoned the camps. But we do have these…

MYLES pulls out some surveillance photographs.

…surveillance photographs taken by the Allies showing air extraction systems. And these construction plans of the camps confirm this, even showing the fake showers placed in the rooms to wrong-foot the victims into thinking they were going to wash. What's more, some of the ventilation systems are still visible in the ruins of the gas chambers.

ELENA disregards the photos. She starts to breathe heavily. She unwraps the inhaler that MYLES bought and takes a puff.

ELENA: I'm bored with these photos you keep showing me.

MYLES: Here are some more.

ELENA: Stop it.

He puts some more photos in front of here.

MYLES: Photos of burning pits in Auschwitz.

ELENA: I don't want to see.

MYLES: Bit too gruesome for you?

ELENA: I…

MYLES: In a single year Krema Two alone could incinerate over a quarter of a million bodies. Plus bodies were burnt in the pits you see before you.

ELENA: These were typhus victims. They were burnt to sterilise the camp against the disease.

MYLES: Wrong. It would be impossible for so many people to die of typhus at the same time. And the Germans were fighting a war, as you say, and couldn't spare the millions of bullets on killing Jews. The very reason they created the gas chambers. An efficient killing-machine. What's more, this was not an official photograph, but taken in secret. It shows men…standing inside a pile of naked bodies, with a pit, smoking and steaming in front of them. Some of the bodies are being dragged into the pit.

ELENA looks at the photo and then returns it to MYLES. MYLES hands another document.

Next, a letter sent to SS General Kammler, dated June 20th 1943 citing the number of bodies that can be disposed of in twenty-four hours as four thousand, seven hundred and fifty-six.

ELENA: Are you finished?

MYLES: Not quite. We talked earlier of eyewitness accounts.

ELENA: Yes. What do you say to that? Paul Rassinier?

MYLES: Interned at Buchenwald. Where no one ever claimed there were gas chambers. He never set foot in Auschwitz-Birkenau or any of the other camps with gassings. (*MYLES turns to a document.*) Unlike this man. This is a quote from the testimony of an eyewitness. I quote. 'As early as autumn 1941 gassings were carried out in a room which held two hundred to two hundred and fifty people, had a higher than average ceiling, no windows and a specially insulated door with bolts like those of an airtight door. This room had a flat roof which allowed daylight through the openings. It was through these openings that Zyklon B in granular form would be poured.' Hans Stark, camp Gestapo.

ELENA: Yes.

MYLES: A member of the Gestapo. Not an inmate. Not a survivor.

ELENA: One man. Probably tortured by the Americans.

MYLES: Tortured? No evidence of any complaint of torture made by any prisoner exists. Here's another testimony.

MYLES turns to a document.

Fritz Klein was a doctor at Birkenau. When questioned at his trial as to how he could reconcile the fact that he had sworn the Hippocratic oath with sending people to their deaths in the gas chamber, the good doctor replied, and I quote: 'I am a doctor and want to preserve life. And out of respect for human life I would remove a gangrenous appendix from a diseased body. The Jew is the gangrenous appendix in the body of mankind.'

Pause.

ELENA: I thought you were on my side.

MYLES: Like I say a prosecuting lawyer will be just as well informed. And he'll have expert after expert lined up to tear your argument to shreds, and far more effectively than I ever could.

ELENA: I don't understand what you're trying / to do, but…

MYLES: You also said there's no mention of gassing in Hitler's rhetoric. You make out that he actually disliked its use.

ELENA: Yes.

MYLES: (*Picking up the file.*) This is a quote from *Mein Kampf.* 'If twelve or fifteen thousand Jews who were corrupting the nation had been forced to submit to poison gas, then the millions of sacrifices made at the front would not have been in vain.'

ELENA: It still doesn't change the fact that no documentation ordering mass murder of the Jews was signed by Hitler.

MYLES: In his final testament, Hitler stated that the world, and I quote here, 'would be eternally grateful to me and to National Socialism for having exterminated the Jews in Germany and central Europe'. And here's Heinrich Himmler in a speech to SS leaders in Poznan in 1943 talking about 'a very grave matter about which we shall never speak publicly…I mean the extermination of the Jewish race'. (*Silence.*) So I think you could quite convincingly argue there was, other than the delousing room, another room.

Pause.

In law, we have 'reasonable doubt'. If the prosecution prove beyond reasonable doubt that there is no way a historian of any calibre could come to the conclusions you come to based of the massive quantity of evidence on this subject, they'll be able to prove you're guilty of malfeasance. Of distortion. Or perversion of facts for political aims and therefore guilty.

Pause.

ELENA: Well. It appears, this morning anyway, you managed to get in the shower.

INTERVAL

Act Two

SCENE ONE

Flat. That evening.

TARA is reading a letter. MYLES comes in with a bottle of red wine and some shopping bags.

MYLES: Got some steaks. And a bottle of pricey red.

TARA: Celebrating?

MYLES: Apologising.

TARA: To me?

MYLES: Well…

TARA: What for? Being a dick?

MYLES: Uhm… Right. So I'll just put these in the fridge.

TARA: Oh a package came for you this morning.

    MYLES stops. Looks concerned. TARA gets the package.

MYLES: Package?

TARA: Oh. Weren't you expecting something?

MYLES: No.

TARA: Right. Well. (*Handing it to him.*) I signed for it.

MYLES: Sorry. (*Finally taking it as though he's handling a bomb.*) Great. Thanks.

TARA: Aren't you going to open it?

MYLES: Yes.

    Pause. TARA sees something is wrong. She takes the wine.

TARA: I'll just open this.

MYLES: Yeah.

TARA goes. MYLES is left with his package. He puts it to his ear. He puts it on the coffee table very carefully. Thinks. Stares at it. Then carefully starts to peel open the wrapping. His breathing increases rapidly. Finally he has opened the package. Gingerly he pulls out a couple of very old hard-backed books, tied with some ribbon. He breathes an enormous sigh of relief. Then he unties the ribbon and flicks through the books. He smiles. Then he starts to smell the books. TARA re-enters with the opened bottle of wine and some glasses. She looks at the books. There is a letter with it, which MYLES reads as TARA picks up one of the books.

TARA: '*The Big Book of Jewish Why?*' (*She looks at the next one.*) '*The Bigger Book of Jewish Why?*' Is that grammatically correct?

MYLES: My Mum sent them. My Dad bought them for me when I was a kid. I never read them. She must have thought I'd be interested. Now.

TARA: She knows?

MYLES: Yes. I haven't told my Dad. It's just not come up. I don't think there's a need to discuss every little thing. You know? It's not that there's a problem.

TARA: OK. (*Beat.*) I got a letter today too. For the problem page. A real one. Some fifteen-year-old girl being bullied really badly so she wants to commit suicide. But I don't think the paper'll publish it.

MYLES: Why not?

TARA: I thought I'd write to her myself. Woman / to woman.

MYLES: It's real. I'd have thought…

TARA: It's supposed to be problems with boyfriends and homework. Suicide's too real.

MYLES: So what the hell's the point of the column? If you're not actually going to print the real letters?

TARA: All right. All right. It's not up to / me, is it?

MYLES: I don't understand why you don't fight for it.

TARA: You ever worked for a tabloid newspaper? You don't rock the boat sunshine or you're out on your arse.

MYLES: But you keep banging on about how bored you are writing that drivel and how you ache to write something real…

TARA: I do.

MYLES: OK. Then maybe you should stir things up. Take a risk for once in your career. I mean I don't know why you don't take the plunge, just go out there and find a good story. You're supposed to be a journalist / aren't you…?

TARA: Because I'm not like you! OK? My life isn't one long crusade. I'm just trying to get on with stuff.

Pause. MYLES and TARA make eye contact for the first time in the scene and hold it.

MYLES: I see.

Beat. MYLES smiles.

TARA: What? Why are you looking at me?

MYLES: Nothing.

TARA: Have I dribbled on myself?

MYLES: No it's just… You do this little curly thing with your mouth when you're furious. I noticed it before.

TARA: Little curly thing?

MYLES: I should call you Elvis.

TARA: You shouldn't.

MYLES: You're blushing. I'm sorry.

TARA: I am not fucking blushing OK?

MYLES: Yes you are, you're almost vermillion.

TARA: God you think you're so…special.

MYLES: Not at all.

TARA: You think you're really hot stuff don't you with your steaks and your pricey red and your why don't you do something with your life.

MYLES: Look I'm sorry if I come across a little pompous. / But I was just…

TARA: I mean, OK, you do have a certain…you know…you do have a certain grumpy arrogant thing that's not unattractive. And you have sort of, of, of, eyes that, I suppose some people would find…intelligent.

MYLES: Listen…

TARA: You've been here for four months, why haven't you tried to shag me?!

Beat. The buzzer goes. Beat.

MYLES: Are you expecting / anyone.

TARA: No. You?

MYLES shakes his head no. TARA presses the intercom.

Hello?

PETE: (*Intercom.*) It's Pete Brody!

TARA: Oh. Hi. Come up.

MYLES: What's he doing here?

TARA: Did you invite him?

MYLES: No.

TARA opens the door.

TARA: Maybe he found out.

MYLES: Found out?

TARA: About what you're doing.

MYLES: (*Lying.*) I told you, it's no problem.

PETE enters. There is an awkward silence.

PETE: Your Mum's got one of her migraines. Chucked me out the house. Told me to come over here, said you'd make me some grub. That's all right isn't it?

MYLES: Oh. Of course.

PETE: Take my coat kid.

TARA: I'll do it. (*Takes PETE's coat, looks for somewhere to hang it, doesn't see anywhere and so chucks it on the couch.*)

MYLES: Why didn't you phone me?

PETE: I did. Your phone's on the blink. You haven't eaten already?

MYLES: (*Checking his phone.*) No. I bought some steaks. Bloody phone, I forgot to pay the bill, they've switched it off.

PETE: T-Bone?

MYLES: What?

PETE: The steak. T-Bone is it?

MYLES: Uh...no, sirloin.

PETE: I like T-Bone.

Beat.

TARA: Would you like some wine?

PETE: I'm not a huge drinker.

TARA: Oh I am.

PETE: Are you? That's nice.

MYLES: I'll see about the food.

71

PETE: Good idea.

MYLES goes. Awkward silence.

TARA: So I got a letter today. For my problem page. This /
girl…

PETE: Don't talk to me about problems. You should see 'em
come in Accident and Emergency.

TARA: Oh right. Well that must be…

PETE: One feller came in yesterday – nights is the worst. So
this feller – real mincer if you see what I'm saying – he
minces in, he's got a carrot…a carrot…stuck up his anal
passage.

TARA: No!

PETE: I says how do you get yourself in this state sunshine? He
says – get this – he says… 'I was pleasuring myself.' Bold
as you like. Looking at me like to say: 'You got a problem
with that have you?' And I'm looking at him, like, I can't
believe the barefaced cheek of it. I mean, make something
up. Lie.

TARA: Well what the hell can you say with a carrot stuck up
your bum?

PETE: Well I don't know do I? 'I was making a salad and I
slipped.'

MYLES enters.

MYLES: Dinner'll be about twenty minutes.

PETE: I'm not hungry.

MYLES: But I just…

PETE: I'm all tense. I was listening to my Talk Radio on the
way over, it's got me all riled up. All knotted up. I couldn't
eat now.

MYLES: You just made me cut up those steaks so there's enough for all of us.

PETE: They were talking about that Nazi. What's her name? You know, that monster that denies the Holocaust.

MYLES: What?

PETE: What's her name?

TARA: Elena Manion?

TARA and MYLES look at each other.

PETE: Right. These people make me laugh. I mean if you think the Holocaust was justified, why spend so much time trying to prove it never happened? Anyway it turns out they're putting her on trial. Good. Throw away the key I say.

MYLES: What did they say?

PETE: Obviously the human rights brigade is up in arms. Your lot.

MYLES: Dad…

PETE: They make me sick. Free speech? We should allow her to say what she wants? I was spitting blood in the Mondeo just now. Then they said – get this – they said her lawyer's a Jewish boy. Defending this – this *animal.* Bet his parents are proud of him, eh? Slogged their guts out to give him an education, now he's shovelling shit in their faces.

MYLES: And if you saw her here in the street, if she'd collapsed in the street, wouldn't you help her? If she came to your hospital. You'd save her life if you had to.

PETE: Her life. Not her ideas. Not her lies. To lie should not be allowed. What if there's this geezer who decides out of nowhere to go round telling people you're a paedophile? And it gets you into trouble. It loses you friends. Your wive leaves you. You lose your job. And it eventually destroys you. Sometimes you have to stop people. You have to just stop them.

TARA: Well...because I mean I understand you, but by protecting the individual's rights...in a way, in an indirect way I suppose, but in a way that's inadvertently protecting all individuals. All minorities. So it's a paradox. By defending this Holocaust denier, this lawyer...this son...is protecting the Jews. So the parents should be proud. Very proud.

PETE: Let me tell you about my Dad, Joe. My Dad he wasn't much for talking. He didn't say anything about his family when I was a boy. I asked him...I pumped him with questions, but he just fobbed me off. Then when he was dying he told me. He told about the last time he saw his parents.

Pause.

Now you got to go back to nineteen thirty-eight. November the ninth. Kristallnacht they call it. The Nazis were confiscating Jewish property. Smashing up shops and homes. Joe and his Mum and Dad and his sisters and his...his baby brother...they were rounded up. They'd... the stormtroopers, they'd built a bonfire out the furniture from the family home and they were all just standing there watching it. Then, sort of suddenly, for no reason, one of the stormtroopers went up to Joe's Mum...she was standing watching the bonfire, clutching her little baby in her arms. They tore the kid from your great-grandmother, she must have been screaming – Joe's father said nothing. Just stared at them as if he was watching a film. Sort of zoned out. They tore the baby from her arms, the kid screaming, the girls screaming, and they threw him on to the fire. Joe didn't scream. He was fourteen, he was copying his Dad. He thought that's what the man does. The man just watches. Just stands there and watches as the little baby burns, and burns and cries its little heart out. Your great-grandmother ran into the fire and tried to save the kid, but they shot her in the back of the head. Laughed as they did it. Had a nice little chuckle. One of the stormtroopers had been wounded. A couple of the Jewish boys from the neighbourhood had come out with metal bars and bits of chair and started whacking the stormtroopers. It took the men a couple of goes to shoot them all. They kept at it. One of the soldiers had broken his arm and was screaming in pain. Joe watched his Dad go and treat the wounded soldier as his baby son sizzled alive on the fire. Fashioned a splint from one of the broken chairs and fixed the soldier up good. The soldier thanked your great-grandfather. Joe was proud. And hopeful. He saw the soldier smile at his father. Then one of the other soldiers came over and said: 'You think this'll get you off the hook, because you helped this man?' Your great-grandfather said, 'I'm a doctor. It's what I do.' The other soldier smiled. The second Nazi to smile at Joe's father in the same day. He smiled a big wide grin. Joe's Dad didn't say a word. And then...the soldier lifted his gun, still grinning, and shot Joe's Dad in the face. (*Pause.*) Joe ran. He managed to get away from them. He never saw his sisters alive again. His last image of them was of the two of them clinging to each other, shivering with terror, pee dripping down Natasha's legs. He went to the house of a friend from school. The parents had always been good to him. They took him in, but only to keep him there so they could get the soldiers to a cart him away. He was taken to Auschwitz. He was lucky, he was young and fit, so they made him work. He was a...what do they call it...when they force them to carry the bodies...

MYLES: A Sonderkommando.

PETE: Yeah. He had to clear the bodies after the gassings. He wore a mask and shovelled all the naked bodies onto carts to take them to these pits. One day he was he was picking up bodies when he saw Natasha's. Her face gaunt and lifeless, contorted in pain and confusion. Gassed. He had to dump her on the back of his cart and wheel her over to the ovens. He dreamt about that face until the day he died. He used to wake up when we were kids…screaming. Screaming like you couldn't imagine. The police came round loads of times. Anyway like I say for years he never talked about it. If I asked about where he came from he'd say, 'We're English now.'

Pause.

MYLES: Dad. There's something I need to tell you.

PETE: Yes?

MYLES: I…thing is I…

The phone rings.

TARA: I'll get it.

TARA answers the phone.

Hello? Who's calling? (*Getting agitated.*) It's a little late, can he call you tomorrow? …Well his phone isn't working… I don't know, I'm not his secretary… (*Getting even more agitated.*) I don't think I am being controlling actually.

MYLES: Tara.

TARA: (*Into phone.*) It's who?

TARA's demeanour changes completely.

Oh.

TARA looks at MYLES fearfully.

MYLES: Who is it?

TARA: It's…uhm…well…it's…

MYLES: Yes?

TARA: I think you'd better…

MYLES: Oh. Right.

MYLES gets the phone.

Myles Brody. (*Pause.*) Yes. I can't talk just at the moment. Can I call you back? OK. Speak to you later

Pause.

PETE: Myles. You wanted to say something?

MYLES: Yeah…yes. Just…you want English mustard or Dijon?

Beat.

PETE: English.

Blackout.

SCENE TWO

Flat. Later that same night.

PETE has gone and the plates and glasses of half-finished wine are still lying around. MYLES picks up the receiver, delves into his pocket for a phone number written on a piece of paper, and dials. He leaves the paper on the table.

MYLES: Myles Brody for Dr Manion please. Thanks. Hi, it's me. Sorry about that I had someone here… Yeah and it turned into a whole big…

TARA enters.

My father. Well my Dad can go on an on once he gets going.

TARA glares at MYLES shocked, MYLES waves her away.

I've been doing some thinking about the case and I want to discuss a strategy.

TARA starts to play with the pieces on the chessboard. She is setting it up, but very slowly because she is distracted by MYLES's phone conversation.

Tomorrow. OK. In the meantime I'll work on it, I'm working on it all the time... Yes. I know. You're very welcome. Yes. Get a good night's sleep.

MYLES puts down the phone. As MYLES turns to look at TARA, she turns away, and back to the chessboard. He stands over her and looks down. He watches her for a moment as she moves the pieces into the start position. Then he notices that the Queens are on the wrong squares and he shifts Queen for King and King for Queen at each end.

TARA: That's very rude.

MYLES: It's wrong. Queens on their colours.

TARA: Should be the other way round.

MYLES: Queen defends the King in chess. The female is the General.

TARA: And she can move this way...

MYLES: (*Showing her.*) Diagonally, horizontally, backwards and forwards. She goes out fighting, killing, building; she'll sacrifice herself to defend her King.

TARA: I can see why you like this game.

MYLES: Shall we play?

TARA: Don't you have to work?

MYLES: I had a good day. Anyway you asked me to teach you.

TARA: No I didn't.

MYLES: Yes. When I first moved in. The first day. (*He sits down.*) You be white.

TARA: You cavalierly offered your services. I didn't / ask.

MYLES: White always gets the advantage.

TARA: I don't need the advantage thanks very much. And I didn't ask.

MYLES: I think you did. Go on. Start. You can either move a pawn or a knight. You know how the knight moves? Yes?

TARA: (*Slightly irritated with his pomposity.*) You mean the little pony?

MYLES: Uh…yes, if you like.

TARA: Like this?

She moves the knight. He moves a pawn.

MYLES: Correct.

She moves a pawn.

Well done.

He moves a pawn.

TARA: (*Moving her bishop.*) Can I do this?

MYLES: Yes. Bishop goes diagonally on its own colour.

TARA: Don't you feel…I mean I know you're a lawyer and you're supposed to be professional and everything, but I'm sorry I don't see…after everything your grandad went through…

MYLES: Tara…

TARA: No, I'm sorry…I don't see…and just now…on the phone just now…

MYLES: (*He moves.*) Could you not listen to my calls please?

TARA: You were talking about avoiding a trial. Is that what you want?

MYLES: Yes.

TARA: Is that really what she deserves? A get-out-of-jail-free card?

MYLES: You don't understand.

TARA: Then talk to me. Tell me.

79

MYLES: I have to stop her coming to trial. I have to prevent her from becoming the celebrity martyr to free speech and anti-political correctness she'd so dearly love to be.

TARA: Prison sounds like the best place for her.

MYLES: In nineteen-twenties Germany this funny little dude with a moustache was put on trial for treason, for starting a political party called the National Socialists. No one gave the guy a second thought before the trial, but he railed and he ranted and became a minor celeb. When they banged him up in Landsberg prison he became a martyr to the Nazi cause and wrote a little number called *Mein Kampf*. So you see if I lose, and she goes to prison, then it'll set the human rights movement back fifty years. She'll be championed by left and right and every libertarian in the middle. She'll be a figurehead for neo-Nazis everywhere and they'll dress it up as the right to freely speak. Whatever it is you have to say must be defended. I believe that. Extreme views can only be given credibility if they're attacked, or banned. You can't put an idea behind bars. You can't put a gag over the mouth of an opinion. It'll find a way of coming back at you even louder. With even more force. Denying the gassing of millions of people is obscene, that's not in doubt. Racism is obscene whichever way it's served up, but it won't go away just because we legislate against it. This woman is fierce and explosive and has an extraordinary recall. She's a brilliant manipulator and she understands how to get a point across. She's not to be underestimated. For all those reasons she mustn't be given a national stage from which to pontificate. Otherwise anything could happen. It's completely counter-productive to try to silence someone who no one took any notice of. Because people will wonder…'Why are they trying to silence her? Maybe she has got something to say.' A neo-fascist, a historical revisionist who'd been rendered comprehensively obsolete, now has a cause. And there's nothing more dangerous than a writer with a cause.

Beat.

TARA: You lied to me.

MYLES: What?

TARA: When you first moved in.

MYLES: I…

TARA: You told me you weren't passionate.

MYLES: I'm not.

TARA: Come on.

MYLES: I'm really not.

TARA: All that stuff about human rights.

MYLES: You're wrong, I'm dispassionate. I have to be, or I lose.

Pause. TARA smiles. She moves her Queen.

TARA: Checkmate.

MYLES stares at the board.

MYLES: What?

TARA: You're a bloody good chess teacher I'll give you that.

MYLES: What happened there?

TARA: I told you, I wouldn't have asked you to teach me.

MYLES: You can play?

TARA: I was captain of chess-soc at school.

MYLES: You totally stitched me up.

TARA jumps up.

TARA: Want the rest of that wine?

She drains the bottle into two glasses.

MYLES: (*Still staring at the board.*) I was sure you asked me to teach you.

TARA: (*Handing him a glass of wine.*) You didn't answer my question.

MYLES drinks the wine still staring at the board. TARA stares at him.

MYLES: Hmm?

TARA: I asked you a question tonight just before your Dad arrived.

MYLES gets up and walks to the other end of the room. He looks through some files.

MYLES: Tara…

TARA: Why haven't you tried it on with me? You're not gay. I know that because gay guys don't look at me / like that…

MYLES: Look I thought we agreed this was inappropriate.

TARA: That's bullshit and you know it.

MYLES: You…up until last night you had a, and I quote, 'very serious' boyfriend, who you loved very much.

TARA: Had.

MYLES: Who, by the way, is built like a truck.

TARA: Is there something wrong with you? Impotency or something?

MYLES: Look I should… There is stuff I need to read…

TARA: Oh yeah right, walk away. Jesus you're unbelievable.

MYLES: Tara…

TARA: You did exactly the same thing to your Dad just now.

MYLES: That's enough.

TARA: You get close to someone. You get close to showing some kind of genuine...to explaining.

MYLES: Excuse me, I don't need to explain anything to anyone actually. And I don't appreciate being interrogated, and whatever it is you're subtly / accusing me of...

TARA: I'm sorry you feel interrogated, but talking to you is like pulling teeth. I'm responsible for both sides of the conversation and it's hellish.

MYLES: Well I'll be moving on soon so you won't have to put up with my objectionable personality much longer.

TARA: Oh of course moving on again...

MYLES: I'm obviously not wanted here...

TARA: Don't be such a complete wanker.

MYLES: I rest my case...

TARA: You're twisting everything I say.

MYLES: Stop reading things into...stop psychoanalysing my life, OK, it's got fuck-all to do with you.

TARA: I...

MYLES: You've written so many agony letters, you think you know something about the way people work. But you're being simplistic. I think you've forgotten that it's coffee-break bullshit. Just because a lot of people read it doesn't mean it isn't just pointless drivel.

TARA: Fine.

MYLES: I'm just reminding you because you seem to have forgotten. You started believing your own crap and that's dangerous.

TARA: Well. Thanks. That's really very considerate of you.

MYLES: Oh come on don't do that...

TARA: No, no, because I was obviously labouring under the false assumption that I had any right to live. Thank you for disabusing me of that idea.

MYLES: Now who's twisting what people say?

TARA: Right.

MYLES: Right what?

TARA: No. It's fine. You want to be like that.

MYLES: Like what?

TARA: You try living with a person...a fucking spectre who passes through your house, with barely a look in your direction. Who...who isn't interested in any kind of human contact...

MYLES: I'm a tenant here. OK? I need a room and a bed and basic facilities and that's all. I don't need a buddy. Or a pal. Or a confidante for late night heart-to-hearts. I need you to be a landlady. I pay you at the end of every month and I use my room and I don't get tangled up in the chaos you refer to as your social life. Is that agreed?

TARA: Just go and fuck yourself Myles! Yeah. Because there's no sign of anyone else offering to fuck you, so you better fuck yourself!

MYLES: You are! You're offering. You practically served yourself up on a platter.

TARA slaps MYLES. He grabs her and pulls her to him and kisses her roughly. She resists at first, but they fall into each other. TARA undoes the belt on his trousers, then she tries to pull them down, when suddenly MYLES pulls away from her violently. Pause. TARA stares at him confused and upset. Silence.

I'm married.

SCENE THREE

Safe-house. Study. The next day.

ELENA is doing her jigsaw. It is far advanced from the last time we saw it. About three-quarters finished. MYLES is there. Both are very agitated now and are having difficulty hiding the fact.

ELENA: So. What's this master plan you wanted to talk about?

MYLES: You know the *Art of War*? Japanese bloke…

ELENA: Sun Tzu. What of it?

MYLES: He said: 'To win without fighting is best.'

ELENA: I'm familiar with the text.

MYLES: There is a way to prevent us going to trial.

ELENA: (*Pause.*) I'm breathless with anticipation.

MYLES: But you're not going to like it.

ELENA: (*Beat. Menacing.*) Try me.

MYLES: Retract your denial of the gas chambers.

Silence. ELENA looks at MYLES, then back down at the jigsaw.

ELENA: (*She slots a piece into the puzzle.*) Look it goes there! I've been trying to fit that somewhere for hours.

MYLES: The CPS will have to drop the case. They'll have to. Win without fighting.

ELENA: Win?

MYLES: Your freedom.

ELENA: And damn myself? Damn my reputation? Three decades' work up in smoke.

MYLES: I understand.

ELENA: And that's the best you can come up with? Take the coward's way out? Retract my book. Destroy my life's work. You'd like that wouldn't you?

MYLES: You couldn't be indicted under the Incitement to Religious Hatred Act…it's a good option…

ELENA: That's hardly the point.

MYLES: Only you can make the decision.

ELENA: I'll never relent. Not while I have truth on my side.

MYLES: The truth?

ELENA: Yes. The truth.

MYLES: As you see it?

ELENA: Man is the measure of all things Myles, or don't you know your Plato?

MYLES: The Attorney General is out for blood. The government has to be seen to be putting a squeeze on racism of every hue.

ELENA: Since when have we allowed the government to get involved with academic pursuit? With the writing of history? It's utterly perverse and I will not stand by to see my great profession violated like this.

MYLES: Most people in your great profession see you as an aberration. A fringe eccentric, an ideologue who distorts historical truth…

ELENA: That's because they don't accept that historical truth isn't stationary. It isn't a lump of igneous rock that sits there unchanging through all eternity. It's always in flux. Like crystals reflecting sunlight. Hindsight means we look at the past through the prism of our current consciousness. As time moves, as we know more, an event alters in meaning, in consequence.

MYLES: I don't doubt that. But the facts remain the same. A thing happened.

ELENA: Well I'm a historian. The event is hardly the end of the matter. It isn't science. There's interpretation, context…

MYLES: Yes, but the idea that its meaning changes through time doesn't alter the fact that a thing happened. That something concrete happened.

ELENA: Look…

MYLES: Look, if I take this piece of your jigsaw.

MYLES picks up a loose piece that is not in a place.

ELENA: Be careful with that.

MYLES: …and I place it in here, look, I slot it in, I force it into a place where it isn't supposed to go.

ELENA: Clearly.

MYLES: And I keep doing that with the other pieces… (*MYLES starts sticking puzzle pieces where they are not meant.*)

ELENA: Stop it you're / ruining it.

MYLES: …and eventually I have a picture. But in forcing the pieces into places they're not meant, I impose a new pattern and so the picture becomes distorted.

ELENA: Dear old Klimt'd be spinning in his grave.

MYLES: But it doesn't change the original picture. It doesn't change the truth of the original picture. And even if we do it with the only copy, and this is the last representation of the Klimt. The original still exists. Where? In the memory? It doesn't matter. It existed. It was – specific… There was a true picture. And that truth doesn't change. And that truth is locked in this mess we now have in front of us for ever.

ELENA: Well…this is an uncharacteristic fit of creative energy for you.

MYLES: 'Man is the measure of all things,' was said by Protagoras. Plato didn't agree with him. He believed in universal truths. Truths that were eternal, that were fixed in time, unchanging. Beauty, Wisdom, Justice…

ELENA: Is this little circus display suppose to have some academic merit?

MYLES: Here's another example.

ELENA: This is my reputation on the line here Mr Brody, and I'll thank you not to make a mockery of it with your kindergarten art demonstration.

MYLES: Imagine we lose the case. I don't like to do that, but one has to prepare for every eventuality in this game.

ELENA: Ridiculous.

MYLES: In fact imagine I completely balls it up and the judge is feeling particularly vindictive; you could get the maximum custodial sentence. Seven years. And your reputation is such – and I mean the racist jibes, the TV appearances those baroque turns on *Newsnight* attacking immigration and multiculturalism with all the venom of an anaconda… So it's hairy at Her Majesty's pleasure and you have to spend most of your time in solitary confinement. And you languish there until your health deteriorates. And you emerge from the prison a broken woman. And we finally get to the appeal courts, and they overturn the decision. Your name is cleared. And you sit in hospital vindicated. The facts are changed, history is rewritten. You're not a criminal. But the memory of your incarceration, the trauma of it is retained in your lungs. In your ravaged body. The event existed. You know that because you have to breathe through a respirator the rest of your life.

Pause.

ELENA: You're wrong, you know. An anaconda isn't venomous. It coils its vast body around you and hugs you to death. While we're in the business of correcting each other.

MYLES: Look…

ELENA: What are you trying to prove anyway with your horror story?

MYLES: That there's more than your reputation at stake here.

ELENA: Thank you for reminding me.

MYLES: Well you don't seem to be taking this seriously.

ELENA: I assure you there's nothing I take more seriously. My life is at stake. But I'll go to prison before I deny what I know to be…what I feel to be…before I destroy my life's work.

MYLES: And what is your life's work? Keeping fascism alive?

ELENA: What?

MYLES: Isn't it the case that by saying the Nazis weren't so brutal you're trying to make them acceptable again?

ELENA: Now you're putting words into my mouth.

MYLES: Is that wrong?

ELENA: Please don't presume to know what I stand for.

MYLES: No. You're too clever to come right out and say it, aren't you?

ELENA: Just because I think the Holocaust is a cynical piece of propaganda doesn't mean I'm a racist.

MYLES: Then prove it.

ELENA: Take Kristallnacht for example.

MYLES: Oh now that didn't happen?

ELENA: A few drunken louts, nothing more. Youthful high jinks. The next day, the *London Times* editorial wrote that

'No foreign propagandist bent upon blackening Germany before the world could outdo the tale of burnings and beatings.'

MYLES: See that's where you're stuck. You're stuck in 1938. You still think Hitler was a good thing. An inspiring leader. A hero.

ELENA: Oh come on, are we really expected to believe that innocent men, women and children were rounded up like cattle and squeezed into train carriages and led to their slaughter? Were hunted like vermin and put down like lice? Were tortured, experimented on and burned?

MYLES: So even after all the evidence is presented to you, all that evidence. You still insist...

ELENA: Yes.

MYLES: How?

ELENA: Because it doesn't make sense. This was the country of Bach and Beethoven, of Goethe and Thomas Mann, of Heisenberg and Schopenhauer. These were the greatest minds in all human history, the most advanced thinkers and artists. Would such people be capable of such barbarity?

MYLES: Apparently. Shall we go over the evidence again? The evidence of the German government, the Munich Institute, the German people themselves now accept. Why can't you?

ELENA: Because it's racist. It's anti-German.

MYLES: Anti-German?

ELENA: These weren't some third world people running around with towels on their heads and hanging about in tribes.

MYLES: Then what are you saying?

ELENA: I've said it. I've explained it to you. How many times do I have to go over it?

MYLES: I want you to say what you really think.

ELENA: If you're so brilliant, why don't you tell me? You're so happy to put words in my mouth.

MYLES: That your life's work is hate. Hate's blinded you. It's ruled everything you've done. It's become your faith.

ELENA: My faith?

MYLES: You know what happened, you know the truth. You know the facts and you twist them to fit your racist agenda.

ELENA: I'm not the racist. I don't make up lies to destroy the memory of others.

MYLES: Who does then?

ELENA: You know who I mean.

MYLES: Tell me. Tell me again.

ELENA: The Jews.

MYLES: Yes. Thank you.

ELENA: They're obsessed with their own annihilation, it's their persona. They have a 'we're so special', a – a…'you can't join our club' mentality. They thrive on struggle and persecution; it's the glue that binds them.

MYLES: But according to you they're not persecuted.

ELENA: I never said that. Stop putting words into my mouth. Of course they've been persecuted. The Spanish Inquisition, the blood libel, the Cossacks, the pogroms. Everywhere they've gone, they've been hounded out. This is a people constantly at odds with the prevailing values. Sitting in Europe ignoring the fact that everyone around them was worshipping Christ.

MYLES: So, hang on, let me get this right…

ELENA: Look, if I was a Jew I would be far more concerned not by the question of who pulled the trigger, but why. Is it something in the water? Is it envy? Or is it part of the endemic human xenophobia? It is human to be anti-Semitic.

MYLES: But you wrote in your book… (*MYLES picks up her book and opens it.*) 'Why make so much of the Jewish tragedy? Genocides have happened all over the world. Do we bat an eyelid over the killing of a million Armenians? What about in Kosovo, in Darfur, in Rwanda? Why are the Jews so special? You can't have one rule for one group and another rule for the others.'

ELENA: Yes.

MYLES: Well which is it? Are the Jews a special case or not?

ELENA: But the Jews wallow in the animosity. The greatest threat to their existence is to be ignored by an indifferent world. They need people like us. If Holocaust deniers didn't exist, they'd have to invent them.

MYLES: So you're doing it as a favour?

ELENA: No I'm doing it to pierce their egos. Their Jew egos. They should never be allowed to feel safe here. Why should they? They think they're cleverer and funnier and holier than everyone else. They take power, they twist facts to their own advantage. They flash their money, the money they squeezed out of the tolerant England that rescued them from destruction yet again. No they must never be allowed to feel safe. To take root. Never.

Pause.

MYLES: I see.

ELENA: Of course, what I mean is…

MYLES: I know what you mean.

ELENA: Myles. I was angry, I, people lash out when they're angry…

MYLES: Do they?

ELENA: Stop it. No one's work can stand up to this kind of scrutiny. No one's life. Can yours?

MYLES: I'm not on trial.

ELENA: It's inhuman.

MYLES: I didn't try and cynically exploit my notoriety to sell a book.

ELENA: That's not true.

ELENA starts to breathe heavily. MYLES reaches for her inhaler and holds it.

MYLES: Admit it. You knew you'd be arrested. That's why you did it.

ELENA: Give me that.

MYLES: Admit it. You must have known it would come to this.

ELENA: I…no…I…I need my…please.

MYLES: That's why you said you'd been expecting the police.

ELENA: I didn't say that…I never said that…

MYLES: You were prepared to risk prison. Your health.

ELENA: I didn't think it would get this far. I never believed…

MYLES: No you thought you'd get a bit of press interest, get yourself back on TV, shift some of your back catalogue…

ELENA: I'm begging you.

MYLES: Get massive publicity for your new book and then they'd drop the case.

ELENA: Lies!

MYLES: That's a hell of a marketing strategy I'll give you that.

ELENA: For God's sake, help me. I couldn't survive in prison. I couldn't handle it. After everything I've said, you're right Myles, the place will be crawling with coons and pakis and who knows what else, when they get their hands on me in there it'll be a massacre. You have to help me Myles. Please. I never raised a hand to hurt a living soul. For Christ's sake don't let them destroy me.

MYLES gives her the inhaler and she sucks on it. Then calms down. Pause.

MYLES: Renounce your book Elena. Renounce your entire catalogue of revisionism. Admit there had to be gas chambers and then crawl back into obscurity where you belong.

ELENA: If I retract what I say than my whole body of work is worthless. Everything I have written will be called into question.

MYLES: Not if new evidence has come to light. That makes you reassess, re-evaluate. The Munich Report for example. The Bad Arolsen documents… History is constantly shifting as you've been arguing.

ELENA: I see.

MYLES: Or stand by your work.

ELENA: And face prison?

MYLES: That's the choice.

Silence. ELENA thinks.

ELENA: It may be too late.

MYLES: Why?

ELENA: A journalist contacted me.

MYLES: A journalist?

ELENA: They phoned this morning.

MYLES: On this number?

ELENA: Demanded an interview. Said it would be of great interest to their readers.

MYLES: I told you not to talk to anyone.

ELENA: I know, but I felt I needed to get my views out. I felt people needed to hear for themselves.

MYLES: When will the article come out?

ELENA: She said tomorrow.

MYLES: Tomorrow?

ELENA: Yes. So you see, it may already be too late.

MYLES: Wait. She?

ELENA: Yes. The girl from the *Daily Mirror*.

MYLES stares at ELENA wildly, realisation dawning on him.

Myles dear boy you look like you've seen a ghost.

SCENE FOUR

Flat. That evening.

TARA, in her dungarees from Scene One and a pair of marigolds on her hands, is on her knees vigorously rubbing a side table with a cloth.

MYLES enters. He stands in the doorway looking at TARA, who continues to dust, despite being aware of his presence.

MYLES: What are you doing?

TARA: You were always complaining about the place being a tip…

MYLES: Right.

TARA: ...so I thought I'd give it a bit of a dust.

MYLES: Tara.

TARA: I'm going to start on the bathroom next, so if you need to get in there...

MYLES: Was it you?

TARA: I mean if you need a shower. Do it first yeah because...

MYLES: Did you phone Elena Manion this morning?

Pause.

Fuck.

TARA: Myles...

MYLES: Just what exactly was going on in that bewildered little brain of yours?

TARA: Can we just talk about this for a moment...

MYLES: No.

TARA: Can't we just discuss it...

MYLES: OK. I want you to stop it.

Beat.

TARA: I...

MYLES: I want you to phone your editor and pull the article.

TARA: I can't.

MYLES: Phone her now.

TARA: Myles. I can't.

MYLES: I'm serious about this.

TARA: It's too late.

Pause.

MYLES: I don't believe this is happening.

TARA: I never mention you.

MYLES: Jesus Christ.

TARA: In the article. I never mention you.

MYLES: Out of what? Loyalty?

TARA: In a way?

MYLES: After you'd gone ferreting through my papers…

TARA: I did not go ferreting through your / papers…

MYLES: How did you get the phone number of the safe-house then?

TARA: I pressed redial.

MYLES: What?

TARA: After you phoned her last night.

MYLES: Amazing.

TARA: Myles…

MYLES: I mean didn't you have any…any qualms about taking the number and using it for your own professional gain?

TARA: Of course I had qualms.

MYLES: After I asked you…after I told you how important… how…

TARA: I know. I'm sorry.

MYLES: After everything I said last night. I'm stunned. I'm actually stunned.

TARA: Please.

MYLES: You stole the number…

TARA: Not exactly stole, / it was…

MYLES: You take into your head to phone up my client, a woman I'm trying to keep from the glare of publicity…

TARA: Myles.

MYLES: And you interview her for a national newspaper.

TARA: Let's sit down. Let's talk.

MYLES: What are we doing now? Aren't we talking now?

TARA: Well no, you're sort of shoutily cross-examining me.

MYLES: I'm just warming up.

TARA: Listen to me.

MYLES: After everything I said last night.

TARA: I know.

MYLES: You've probably ruined this whole case.

TARA: Why?

MYLES: Because, you birdbrain, I was trying to get her to re-… It doesn't matter. Fuck. I can't believe you did this… FUCK!

MYLES grabs the bottle of wine on the side table and smashes it.

TARA: Jesus you've cut your hand.

MYLES: Shit.

TARA: Hold on.

TARA runs off. MYLES stands there holding his hand.

MYLES: Bollocks.

TARA comes back with a first aid kit.

TARA: Show me.

MYLES shows his hand.

All right. I need to clean it.

TARA gets out some antiseptic and some cotton wool.

MYLES: Wait. That'll hurt won't it.

TARA: Stop moaning.

TARA dabs the antiseptic onto the cotton wool.

MYLES: Do you even know what you're doing?

TARA: No.

TARA wipes MYLES's hand with the cotton wool. He screams in pain.

MYLES: God that hurts.

During the next part TARA amateurishly bandages MYLES's hand.

TARA: You really don't understand anything do you. You're so clever. You're such a brilliant lawyer...

MYLES: Don't try and talk your way out of this.

TARA: Talk? You don't talk you lecture. You fulminate. You bang on and on about freedom of speech and human rights and you keep this woman locked up. Away from the press. Away from the world.

MYLES: She's... I can't believe I have to explain / this to you...

TARA: This isn't a dictatorship with you as the great benevolent ruler to determine what's good for the people.

MYLES: That's not an excuse for what you did.

TARA: No. This is. You're a hypocrite. You wax lyrical about freedom of expression and how you can't stifle ideas...you lie to your father...

MYLES: I didn't lie...

TARA: I was confused at first. About why you were working so hard to defend this woman. This woman who was obviously a little deluded at best, at worst…God at worst, what is she at worst? I dread to think.

MYLES: That's not relevant.

TARA: And you talked about preventing her from becoming a martyr.

MYLES: Which you destroyed by publishing…

TARA: But it didn't explain why you'd kept your Dad in the dark.

MYLES: Careful.

TARA: Knowing what you know.

MYLES: It's complicated.

TARA: I was up all last night after Pete told that story about your grandfather…

MYLES: You're on really thin ice here Tara…

TARA: And the only conclusion I could come to was that you were hiding her from him. That you were trying to protect him.

MYLES: Yes.

TARA: But you couldn't see it was yourself that you were protecting.

MYLES: So I'm a coward.

TARA: No.

MYLES: I'm a selfish coward.

TARA: No.

MYLES: But I didn't just fuck someone over to further my career.

TARA: That's not what I did.

MYLES: No?

TARA: People have a right to know.

MYLES: People?

TARA: Yes. People. Your Dad. People.

MYLES: (*With derision.*) People?

TARA: See you can't even keep the contempt out of your voice.

MYLES: What?

TARA: Admit you don't trust people. That you look down on them. That you think they're easily led. That they believe any crap that's served up to them.

MYLES: I never said that…

TARA: You were the one who was enchanted by her. Because…I don't know why…because of what she represents. You're the one who's obsessed by her. The rest of us just see a very strange old loony.

MYLES: That's too simplistic…

TARA: When you read the article you'll see for yourself. She's not a martyr. She's not a leader. She's an antiquated racist who no one takes seriously. You didn't have enough faith in us Myles. You didn't trust us to think for ourselves. You didn't even trust the judicial system that you kept telling me was extraordinary and / fair and…

MYLES: Please don't talk to me about the judicial system…

TARA: I know how you feel about what she stands for and you're right to be horrified and defensive, but you don't have the right to control the information. What happened, what she denies, this is all our histories, not just yours. We're all implicated in this. We're all survivors of the Nazis. This is the worst thing humanity can do to itself. Destroy people's dignity, then their lives, then deny their suffering. It's a triple death.

Pause. TARA finishes up the bandage.

You're done.

MYLES: Thanks.

TARA: Myles. What happened to your marriage?

MYLES: I told you it's complicated…

TARA: Why didn't you tell me about her?

MYLES: It's difficult…

TARA: You hurt me.

MYLES: I'm sorry.

TARA: We're under siege every day. Plots and terror and conspiracy theories. Comment. Debate. I've never had so much information and I've never felt so helpless. And you…the way you talked. You were so sure. So clear. So eloquent. When I heard you speaking about how we should air things openly I was mesmerised by your conviction. I was your apostle.

MYLES: Tara…

TARA: But you say one thing and you do another and then you treat me like a child. To be patronised.

MYLES: I didn't mean to do that.

TARA: Then tell me.

Pause.

MYLES: Anna and I…we got married young. She is Jewish and so when I was approached to defend Elena she couldn't deal with it. But I couldn't turn it down. I felt compelled to do it. It was the first time my sense of myself had been…I don't know…questioned. Challenged. I had to take it on.

TARA: So you left your wife to take on a case?

MYLES: Things were never right between us. I was using the case as an excuse. I never felt…that…thing with Anna. Do you understand? That…connection.

Pause.

TARA: Yes. I understand.

Pause.

Look, I know…I know I broke a contract between us the moment I dialled that number. But I was so angry.

MYLES: Look…

TARA: There's real evil in the world. And horror and terror and suffering and pain, but there's also you and me and this room and the thing that happens to my heart when you touch me. Myles what I'm trying to say…

MYLES: I've found somewhere else.

TARA: Oh.

MYLES: It's in Queen's Park.

TARA: Right. Queen's Park. Sort of Kilburn, West Hampstead borders…

MYLES: It's just temporary.

TARA: Of course.

MYLES: A friend of mine got seconded to San Francisco, so I can use his flat. I wouldn't be sharing.

TARA: No. Of course. If that's how you feel.

Pause.

I won't hold you to your month's notice. I'll let you break that contract. Call it even.

MYLES: Yeah.

MYLES goes.

TARA is deflated.

SCENE FIVE

Safe-house. Study. A few days later.

ELENA is sitting staring out.

MYLES: I've instructed your new solicitor.

ELENA: The laburnum tree is shedding its blossom. Potts says it's early for the time of year. Potts blames global warming. Thinks the tree's been fooled into thinking it's early autumn when it's actually summer. Marjoram told him to shut up.

MYLES: I'm Jewish.

Pause.

I felt I should tell you…

ELENA: I see.

MYLES: Before I go. I thought you should know.

ELENA: In the interests of full disclosure as they say.

MYLES: If you like.

ELENA: Hmm.

MYLES: Well. Don't you have anything to say? Aren't you shocked?

ELENA: Not really.

MYLES: I don't believe you.

ELENA: I knew.

MYLES: You knew?

ELENA: Yes. Why do you think I hired you?

MYLES: Because I'm Jewish?

ELENA: Of course.

MYLES: I see. A lot of men are advised to hire women lawyers in divorce cases. It doesn't help them. The judges see through it.

ELENA: No. I mean because Jews are good lawyers. Very Machiavellian.

MYLES: Actually I get my brains from my Mum. She's Irish. A lot of her family were lawyers.

Pause.

ELENA: Oh.

MYLES: My Dad's family aren't that bright to be honest.

ELENA: So you're only half Jewish. On your father's side?

MYLES: Yes.

ELENA: Correct me if I'm wrong, but in the eyes of Jewish law aren't you technically a…what is that quaint little word they have for it…a goy?

MYLES: Well…

ELENA: So you're really neither here nor there are you? Not part of the tribe, not really a gentile. You're a bit in limbo.

MYLES: You think you can read me?

ELENA: I think you lied about who you were. Denied your heritage. Were you ashamed?

MYLES: No, I…

ELENA: It's understandable I suppose.

MYLES: You astound me.

ELENA: I'm glad I can still shock you. After everything, I count that as a singular triumph.

MYLES: What a manipulative, merciless, terrifying piece of machinery you are.

ELENA: Thank you.

MYLES: My business here is over.

ELENA: Wait.

MYLES: What?

ELENA: You can't just walk out on me like this.

MYLES: Elena...

ELENA: You can't just leave me high and dry. You have a duty. A fiduciary duty.

MYLES: Your new lawyers are extremely able...

ELENA: We have a contract.

MYLES: Which you broke when you spoke to the press.

ELENA: Why make much of a silly little article?

MYLES: The article isn't the point.

ELENA: What is the point? That people find out what I think? There's nothing new in that. I'm published. I'm talked about. I've been on TV. People may not like what I say but at least they know where I stand. Can you say the same?

MYLES: That's not what this is about.

ELENA: Then what is it about?

MYLES: I'm not having this / conversation...

ELENA: Come on Myles, what is this really about? You want me to retract my work to save myself? To avoid prison for the good of my health? I'm many things, but I'm not a coward. I don't run from the hard things. At least I can say that. At least I stand up to be counted. Every society needs its hate figures. I told you hate binds people. If a person doesn't stand up to fill that position they'll pick someone. The Jews? The immigrants? The blacks? The gypsies? The queers? No. Let them throw stones at me. I'll be the one.

MYLES: Very admirable.

ELENA: The whole thing's ridiculous and hypocritical. That I
should be on trial for speaking my mind. It's an outrage.
While Blair and Bush are gadding about like pompous
peacocks pretending that Iraq had weapons of mass
destruction so they could carpet bomb the place back to
the middle ages. And now we know they were lying, but
are they on trial? Not a bit of it. Not only are they not on
trial, but they're re-elected. We live with lies every day.
Big ones and small ones. We process them. We tuck them
under the carpet. We shrug them off as necessary evil,
realpolitik. This is how the world works. Our government
and our media create a tapestry of lies and people are
dazzled into submission. And they call me a denier. The
whole country's in denial.

MYLES: You know what really sticks in my throat about
you? It's not the pervasive anti-Semitism, or the lies or
the racism or the ignorance or the turning history into
fiction. No. It's that you make the standards of things go
down. Instead of searching for the truth against all the
odds you say this is the truth I want to find and I'll subvert
any theory, I'll twist any fact to make my version fit. It's
dangerous. It's reducing our achievements as humans. It's
making us less. It's denigrating our potential. That's what is
so harmful. We're full of potential. The real evil in all this
bile is denying our potential to be better. To go deeper. To
reach further.

Pause.

Good luck with the trial. You'll need it.

MYLES exits.

ELENA is left alone. Her victory suddenly feels very hollow.

SCENE SIX

Flat. The next day.

PETE stands with a bundle of stuff similar to the one he had when we first saw him in Scene One. MYLES is flexing his hand – it is in some pain and bandaged poorly. There is a box beside him with stuff in it. Books, CDs, papers.

MYLES: Thanks for doing this.

PETE: I got the day off.

MYLES: Yeah.

PETE: You didn't think of calling Anna?

MYLES: Dad…

PETE: She's a wonderful person, she'd understand.

MYLES: (*Picking up a box.*) Get the other end of this would you?

PETE: What ever it is that happened between you, I mean you been together so long.

MYLES: It's heavy.

PETE: I don't understand it.

MYLES plops the box back down with a groan. PETE notices MYLES has a bandaged hand.

What's up with your hand son?

MYLES: It's nothing.

PETE: You can't walk around town looking like that. Give it here.

MYLES: Dad.

PETE: This is a cock-up if ever I saw one, what did they think they were doing, wrapping a take-away pickle?

Enter TARA with a T-shirt.

Who's the schmendrik that bandaged this hand up for you?

MYLES: (*Noticing TARA.*) I did it. I'm the schmendrik. OK?

TARA looks at him.

TARA: This yours?

MYLES: Yeah.

TARA: I'll put it in the box.

MYLES: Thanks.

PETE: Hold your hand out.

MYLES: Dad it's fine.

PETE: Come on. Like this.

MYLES does as he's told. PETE starts to unwrap the bandage.

TARA: I'll put the chess pieces in their boxes for you.

MYLES: You don't have to.

TARA: It's fine. Speed things up.

TARA begins to place all the chess pieces in a box.

PETE: Want to tell me what happened?

MYLES: (*Worried, looking at TARA.*) What?

PETE: With your hand.

MYLES: Oh. I cut myself.

PETE: On purpose?

MYLES: I was cutting vegetables.

PETE: What kind?

MYLES: What?

PETE: What vegetable?

MYLES: I...carrots. OK?

PETE: OK.

PETE examines the hand.

Cutting carrots you say?

MYLES: Yes. Now can you just...

PETE: What were you cooking?

MYLES: What?

PETE: With the carrots?

MYLES: A...I don't know, a stew.

PETE: A stew?

MYLES: Dad.

PETE: I didn't know you made stews.

MYLES: Well. There's a lot you don't know about me.

TARA spins around and goes off. PETE picks a shard of glass out of MYLES's hand.

Ah.

PETE: What's this? Glass?

MYLES: I...

PETE: You think I haven't seen a thousand cuts like this in A and E?

MYLES: OK.

PETE: Want to tell me the truth?

MYLES: I told you. It was an accident. It's fine.

PETE: I know why you're leaving.

MYLES: What?

PETE: I know. I'm not an idiot.

MYLES: Well...yeah but...

PETE: I read her article in the *Mirror*. With the Holocaust denier.

MYLES: Oh.

PETE: What a disgrace. And you living under her roof.

MYLES: Dad...

PETE: And after everything I told her the other night...

MYLES: Yeah but look...

PETE: Must have made you sick to the stomach. I'd be off as well. Like a bullet.

MYLES: It wasn't...

PETE: See, that's why we'll never be completely settled here. There'll always be an element. I taught you that at an early age kid.

MYLES: Yeah but Dad...

PETE: I mean what is that girl thinking interviewing that old cow? The likes of her'll never understand the Jewish struggle. Had it too easy. See that's why we got to stick together.

MYLES: Maybe she thought we should hear the arguments and make up our own minds

PETE: And let people like that rant.

During this next part PETE re-bandages MYLES's hand.

MYLES: I grew up with you ranting and raving. I put up with it. I filtered out the rubbish and kept the good.

PETE: But you're not thinking about the survivors who have to read this filth.

MYLES: I am

PETE: And there's something even more important than that. It insults the memory of the dead. There's an old Jewish custom called Hesed Shel Emet.

MYLES: Yeah it's taking care of the dead. And it's the most genuine act of charity because the people we're helping can't ever repay us.

PETE: Right. Yes. Since when do you know so much about Jewish stuff all of a sudden? All my life I kept banging on about Jewishness and you were never interested.

MYLES: You married Mum. I'm not Jewish.

PETE: Myles…

MYLES: And you've tried to pass the burden on to me and I don't know what to do with it Dad. It's too much. It's not who I am.

PETE: Who are you then?

MYLES: I'm me. Just me.

PETE: And if the Nazis came…

MYLES: Yes, yes, if the Nazis came again I'd be rounded up.

PETE: You think it couldn't happen again?

MYLES: Which is why we should reserve our accusations for real anti-Semites, not ordinary people with no hate in their hearts.

PETE: Here's what I'd like to ask all those people who have a pop at Jews. That would rather we shut up and lay down and die. I'd like to ask them to imagine the world without the Ten Commandments. Without the rule of law. Without the Theory of Relativity. I'd like them to imagine a world without George Gershwin or Kandinsky or Stravinsky or the Marx Brothers or Hollywood. A world without psychoanalysis or *West Side Story* or Mahler's Ninth or T Rex. A world without Sergeant Bilko or Ali G or Larry David or *Little Britain*. Without Inspector Clouseau or

'Somewhere Over the Rainbow' or *Annie Hall.* Imagine no Bob Dylan, no Harold Pinter, no *MASH*, no quantum physics, no jeans, no lipstick, no pill. You wanna live without all those things? Get rid of the Jews. Otherwise leave us the Hell alone and let us get on with civilisation.

TARA re-enters. She carries some CDs. MYLES looks at her.

TARA: I think these are yours. Coldplay. Snow Patrol.

MYLES: Right.

TARA: They were in my stereo. I'm listening to this crap now. (*To PETE.*) See what your son's done to me.

PETE: I want to ask you a question.

TARA: Me?

PETE: That's right.

TARA: OK.

PETE: What were you thinking interviewing that woman, whilst my son is living under your roof. Don't you have any respect?

MYLES: Dad…

TARA: It's OK Myles.

PETE: You think it's right to give that woman air-time? All those impressionable people reading it? You think that's right?

MYLES: I was the lawyer.

Pause.

PETE: What's that?

MYLES: I was the lawyer. For Elena Manion. That's how Tara got to her. I was defending her in her upcoming trial. But I've left. We had a disagreement. There's nothing more I can do for her.

Pause.

I never felt Jewish until I met her. I never felt anything much. She attacked something that was in my core. She activated it. What I do with it now...I have no idea.

Pause.

I don't... The only thing is I don't want you to hate me. I know you'll be disappointed...

PETE: Right. Right. Anyway I'll get this stuff...

MYLES: Is that it? Aren't we gonna...

PETE: You left you say? You're finished?

MYLES: Yes.

PETE: Nothing to talk about then is there?

MYLES: Wait.

PETE: What?

MYLES: I don't know, can't we...I...*talk.*

PETE: Talk?! Now you want to talk?

MYLES: Dad...

PETE: I'll be waiting for you in the van. Don't be long.

PETE picks up the stuff he had at the top of the scene, puts it on the big box MYLES was struggling with before, picks it all up with an enormous heave and goes to the door.

MYLES goes to his last smaller box. The one he came with at the top of the play. He takes out the books his mother sent earlier. He picks them up and looks at them. Tears well up in his eyes. He cries.

He rubs his eyes.

TARA: Is this Arctic Monkeys CD yours?

MYLES: What?

TARA: The Arctic Monkeys. I can't remember.

MYLES: I think so.

TARA: Are you sure?

MYLES: Do you want it?

TARA: I'll put it in the box.

MYLES: If you want it, keep it.

TARA: No. I don't like it anymore.

MYLES: I remember buying it. Maybe I bought it for you.

TARA: I don't think you did.

MYLES: No?

TARA: I don't think so. Anyway, I've gone off them.

MYLES: Really?

TARA: It was too much. All the hype. Everyone banging on about the Arctic Monkeys this, the Arctic Monkeys that, the Arctic Monkeys will save civilisation. Now they're just an annoying load of brats. I've had it with them.

Pause.

So I'll put it in the box then shall I?

MYLES: Whatever.

TARA puts the CD in the box.

Silence. MYLES puts on his coat.

So…

TARA: Right.

MYLES: I might have left stuff…

TARA: Anything I find I'll…

MYLES: Great.

TARA: ...forward it on.

MYLES: Thanks.

TARA: Harrington Gardens.

MYLES: Harridge.

TARA: Harridge. Sorry.

MYLES: It's OK.

TARA: Be all right on your own will you?

MYLES: I'll cope.

TARA: Will you?

MYLES: Yes.

> *TARA zips up his coat.*

TARA: It's cold still. D'you know how to use the heating in Harrington Gardens.

MYLES: Harridge.

TARA: I never get that right.

MYLES: Tara.

TARA: Yes?

MYLES: I...I'm frozen.

TARA: You're...

MYLES: I'm frozen to the spot.

TARA: Oh.

MYLES: I can't move.

TARA: That's odd.

> *They stare at each other.*

MYLES: I don't know what to say.

TARA: Then don't say anything.

Silence.

The buzzer goes off.

END

Acknowledgements

The author would like to thank Greg Ripley-Duggan, Anthony Clark, Frances Poet and Rose Cobbe, without whom this play could not have come into existince.

Also: Diana Hardcastle, Nick Fletcher, David Horovich and Emma Cunniffe.